The Language Teacher Rebel

Teach Yourself ®

The Language Teacher Rebel

A guide to building a successful online teaching business

Dr Anneli Beronius Haake

First published in Great Britain by Teach Yourself in 2021
An imprint of John Murray Press
A division of Hodder & Stoughton Ltd,
An Hachette UK company

1

A CIP catalogue record for this title is available from the British Library

Trade Paperback ISBN 978 1 529 38177 1

eBook ISBN 978 1 529 38175 7

Typeset by KnowledgeWorks Global Ltd.

Printed and bound in Great Britain by Clays Ltd, Elcograf S.p.A.

John Murray Press policy is to use papers that are natural, renewable and recyclable
products and made from wood grown in sustainable forests. The logging and
manufacturing processes are expected to conform to the environmental regulations of the
country of origin.

John Murray Press
Carmelite House
50 Victoria Embankment
London EC4Y 0DZ

www.teachyourself.com

Table of Contents

Meet the Author

I'm Anneli and I'm a Language Teacher Rebel. My mission is to build bridges and encourage cultural integration through online language teaching, and my passion is helping people across the globe to learn about Swedish language and culture through modern technology. I've taught over 20,000 hours of Swedish to over 400 students at all levels across the world for over 15 years.

Beyond setting up and running a successful online Swedish school (Swedish Made Easy), where I help Swedish language students to improve their Swedish, revise for Swedish language exams, and prepare them for moving to Sweden, and writing a course book (*Teach Yourself Complete Swedish*), I've translated a number of books and articles for Swedish universities, worked as a Swedish subtitler for films, and as a language tutor at Middlesex University for its BA Interpreting and Translation students. I am particularly interested in the musical aspect of language (which led me to a PhD in music psychology) and have a teaching degree from Sheffield University in the UK. I'm also an examiner for the SWEDEX (Swedish language proficiency test) and one of the creators of the online course Speak Like a Swede (shortlisted at the Digital Education Awards 2020). I have been featured in numerous media outlets, including the BBC and the *Guardian*, and worked with institutions such as Örebro University, Lund University, Jönköping University and STIM, as well as large multi-nationals including Abercrombie & Fitch, E.ON and Spotify and various language agencies.

I am based in Brighton, UK but I was born and bred in Sweden (Stockholm and Dalarna) and lived there until I was 25. When

I am not being a Language Teacher Rebel, I make music (in the music project Janis), travel when I can, and board dogs with my husband in Brighton.

Acknowledgements

Thanks to my amazing husband Paul Brown for believing in me every step of the way, supporting me, inspiring me, guiding me, motivating me and cheering me on.

Thanks to Frances Quinn, Rafael Argenton Freire (from modernportuguese.com), Farah Aden (from letstalklanguages.com), Ruth Andrés García and John Brown for reading and giving useful and constructive feedback at crucial stages throughout the development of this book.

Thanks to Emma Green and Sarah Cole, for giving me the opportunity, the support and for believing in me.

Thanks to family and friends for listening to my rants and being there, always.

And above all, thank you to all my students throughout the years. You know who you are. I feel privileged to have been your teacher, but in reality, you've taught me more than you will ever know.

How this book works

This book is partly a manual, partly a reference book and partly a manifesto. Feel free to read it cover to cover, or jump straight into something that you're interested in. The first chapter sets the scene for why Language Teacher Rebels are needed now, and why now is the perfect time for you to become one. The second chapter deals with mindset, because as business owners we can't separate our business ventures from our mindsets. Chapter 3 gives you some ideas for products and services that you may want to develop, and Chapter 4 deals with the very important question of how to find your unique niche as an online language teacher. Chapter 5 gives you an overview – the Language Teacher Rebel Roadmap – of how you could go about setting up your business. And the rest of the book deals with these steps in separate chapters, so that by the end of the book, you will have a clear idea of how to set up your own successful online language-teaching business.

This is not an academic book that teaches you how to teach or covers pedagogical methodologies. Rather, it's an accessible resource aimed at those who have an existing language skillset and want to use this for good; be that native speakers wanting to do something new, existing teachers in a school or language centre, recent language graduates, and more. The book does not go into step-by-step technicalities such as how to set up a website, or how to connect a Lead Magnet to a landing page, but will instead guide you through the steps you need to take to build up a robust business infrastructure and create marketing material. I also mention various tools and programs that I've personally found useful and am using at the time of writing. However, bear in mind that when it comes to IT and other technology, alternative platforms are often available, and things change all the time. And you may of course find other tools and programs that work better for you and your business. To see all the tools and programs that I use in my business, and for information and guidance about specific technical steps, go to annelihaake.com. Please note that it is your responsibility to check any legal and financial matters that relate to your own business.

Each chapter starts with an introduction to a particular topic, guides you through the topic in manageable chunks, and then ends with a summary of key takeaways. There's a checklist you can refer to throughout the book to track where you are on your Language Teacher Rebel journey, and a glossary at the end of the book provides definitions for common technical acronyms.

The Language Teacher Rebel Toolkit

As a separate, complementary resource, and to save you time, I have created *The Language Teacher Rebel Toolkit*. This kit includes editable invoice templates, price increase email scripts, an income tracker, profit & loss calculator, course price calculator, social media planner, lesson log template, cancellation email scripts, weekly planner and more. Basically, everything you need to get organized and start teaching is in this *Language Teacher Rebel Toolkit*. You can buy the toolkit separately at www.library.teachyourself.com and *The Language Teacher Rebel Toolkit* icon in this book will show you where there is a relevant *Language Teacher Rebel Toolkit* resource that you can refer to.

Introduction

Language Teacher Rebel (noun): Someone
who wants to use digital technology to make
a difference in the world through helping
people learning a language.

I'm a Language Teacher Rebel. I run my own business as a
language teacher, and I work from home. Or from anywhere
that has a Wi-Fi connection. I set my own hours and my own
rates. I teach, I create and sell material, and I interact with
people online from all over the world.

All of this has been possible because of digital technologies
and the era we now live in. Things have changed. As recently
as 2020 during the COVID-19 pandemic, we saw dramatic
shifts towards working from home using cloud computing in
many countries around the world.

I started teaching Swedish before Skype had gone mainstream
and was only in its infancy. I was studying at university, and I
took on a couple of students – the idea of teaching Swedish
was so much more appealing to me than working in a pub,
which is what I had considered doing.

Since then, I have taught individuals and groups online while
based in the UK, Sweden and the US. My students have
come from all over the world, into my computer, across time
zones and space.

I have taught Swedish conversation, grammar, pronunciation, culture and quirks. My students have shared their life stories with me, taught me their culture, shared their experiences. We have seen the fruits of their labour together (sometimes it has been hard) and I am so proud of their progress. Like the first time they asked a Swede something on the street and got a Swedish reply back. When they first watched a Swedish movie without subtitles. When they read their first Swedish book. Or managed their job interview in Swedish. And then got employed. When they started speaking Swedish more regularly with their partner. All these moments have been so rewarding for us both. And all this has taught me that:

- Language builds bridges.
- Language builds cultural understanding.
- Language is integration.

This is what being a Language Teacher Rebel is all about!

Before getting started on how to become a Language Teacher Rebel and set up your own online language-teaching business, I wanted to mention a couple of practicalities that you may find useful to think about straight away.

✳ Online language teaching as a side gig

We all need enough money to live comfortably. Work out how much you require, set yourself a time frame and a plan to reach that goal. If you can't survive financially for a while without a job, a better method is to start (as I did) by running your language business as a side gig.

A side gig is a business you set up alongside your normal job. This allows you to start small and try it out. Your business can grow organically, while you learn as you go along. Then, if you feel that you have sufficient income from your side gig and things are going well, you can take the step to turn it into a full-time job.

You may need to join a course, a program, or work with a business coach to learn the skills and get the guidance needed to fast-track your personal and business development. You may want to set a milestone to decide whether your business is working or if it's time to tweak things, change direction, or scrap the plan altogether.

The most important thing when you're doing a side gig is to find time for your side gig. Here are six steps for how to do it.

1. IDENTIFY BLOCKED-OUT TIMES DURING YOUR WEEK

Grab a piece of paper (or create an Excel spreadsheet) and write down the days of the week (Monday to Sunday) and all 24 hours of the day, as a calendar. Start by blocking out all the hours of the day when you have commitments. If you work 8 a.m. to 4 p.m., block that out, and include any time it takes for you to get to and from work. If you have children who need to be picked up from school, or any other family commitments, block those out too.

2. MAKE ADJUSTMENTS TO YOUR BLOCKED-OUT TIMES

Ask yourself if you are able to make any adjustments to your blocked-out times. Can someone else take over responsibility for something you are doing? Can you rotate with someone? Could you start and leave work earlier (or later)? Could you take a longer lunch break? Get creative and see where you are able to tweak things. If you can make adjustments, fill them in on your calendar.

3. ADD LIFESTYLE AND HEALTH BLOCKS

Make sure to add at least seven or eight hours of sleep, as well as time for exercising. Block out mealtimes and add in blocks for rest.

4. IDENTIFY WHEN YOU CAN WORK ON YOUR SIDE GIG

Look at your calendar. How much time is left? You might see some time early in the mornings or later in the evenings, perhaps some time at lunch too.

5. ASK YOURSELF: HOW DO I FEEL ABOUT THIS?

Now is the time to honestly reflect on how this makes you feel. Think about what trade-offs you are willing to make to give yourself more time for work without sacrificing all the other things that matter to you. Perhaps you can go for a 30-minute run instead of spending an hour in the gym. Maybe you could get up one hour earlier? Or spend Saturday mornings working on your business? Of course, you shouldn't trade off all your personal activities, but you can probably make some slight adjustments. If you are happy with the time you have, then great! Don't make any adjustments.

6. STICK TO YOUR SCHEDULE AND PROTECT YOUR SIDE-GIG TIME

Once you have carved out some time for your side gig, it's really important to stick to it and not let it slide. Protect your

time, and make sure you use it. Put your calendar somewhere
you can see it or set reminders on your phone, so you don't
forget. Put your phone on silent while you are working
so you don't get distracted. If you live with someone, it's
important to tell them when you're working, so that they
respect your time.

⊗ Money

Now is a good time to set up a simple spreadsheet for the
year, with every month on a different tab. On this spreadsheet,
record your income and expenses (as well as dates for each
income or expense), so you can easily see what you have
made each month. Your taxable amount is your income minus
your expenses. Next, work out your break-even points. Your
business break-even point is what you need to bring in from
your business to cover any expenses that the business has (cost
for a website, a booking system, etc.). Your personal break-
even point is what you need to bring in after tax in order to
cover all your personal outgoings, for example rent/mortgage,
food, electricity, and so on. I have included my Income
Tracker in *The Language Teacher Rebel Toolkit*.

Another thing to do is to set up a savings account and start
putting 10 per cent of your earnings into it. Start straight
away. By doing so, you will feel more comfortable about
making business investments down the line, as you are
building up a financial safety net at the same time. Don't
touch this money; let it accumulate. Don't use it for any part
of your business. You could set it up as a stocks and shares
account (perhaps as a managed balanced portfolio, so you
don't have to think about what exact shares you have), but
even just a savings account will do for now.

You have to take care of the part of your brain that needs to feel safe. You will feel more relaxed and comfortable with a savings account you are contributing to while focusing on your business development.

Now that we've addressed these practical aspects, let's get stuck into how you can become a Language Teacher Rebel!

1

Why now is the perfect time to become a Language Teacher Rebel

Times have changed

In the past, being a language teacher meant working in a physical school or classroom environment. The school would advertise their courses and students would turn up and enrol in a course. If you were a private tutor, you could put up a note or leave a flyer somewhere, or maybe put an ad in a newspaper. A student would contact you and you would either arrange to go to their home, or they would come to yours, or to another physical place where you would have your lessons. Teaching involved commuting, and you were restricted to finding students in the nearby area that were willing to travel to you, or vice versa.

This also meant that students who lived somewhere remote couldn't enrol in courses or have lessons with a private tutor. Instead, they were restricted to audio courses (cassettes or CDs) or studying from a book. They were not able to have direct interaction with a teacher. The digital era has changed that. Geographical boundaries have been broken down.

Today, you can sit at home in Spain and teach someone in Canada. You can collaborate with others through the internet, log on to your teaching schedule, send emails, design and post content, check your bank account, record and upload videos, all from your smartphone or laptop.

The Digital Age has given us incredible opportunities to create content. You can publish articles online, create digital images and visual aids, record videos on your smartphone and upload them to the internet, all for free. You can host live shows on social media platforms for free. You can create podcasts and broadcast them for free. As a Language Teacher Rebel, you're not just a teacher. You're also a business owner, an artist, a designer and a presenter. By using a smartphone, a laptop or a tablet, together with an internet connection, it's possible to reach people from almost every corner of the world.

But don't people just self-study now?

Some think that there's no place for teachers any more. Anyone can self-study, right?

Students today have endless opportunities to learn a language, compared to before. They can use apps, watch online videos, listen to podcasts and audio books. They can join online community groups and connect with others learning the same language. They can follow hashtags and accounts on social media platforms about the language they're studying. They can watch TV and movies and listen to radio. They can join language-learning webinars. And they can do all of this from home, while sipping a cup of coffee. Or at their workplace. Or even while travelling. It's really quite incredible to think about the many opportunities that students have today, even compared to just 10–15 years ago.

Yet, most students still want to be taught by a teacher. Why? The answer can be narrowed down to three things:

(1) structure, (2) motivation and accountability, and (3) personal interaction.

Let's start with **structure**. Just because we have access to a lot of free information on the internet doesn't mean we know how to structure a process. This is especially true for a longer process such as language learning. Watching short video clips on a particular grammar point may help to solve a particular problem, but it does not help to structure a learning process to guide a student who wants to go from level A1 to A2, for example. Self-study requires students to essentially create their own study plan, which is a huge undertaking for most people. It also takes a lot of time that most people don't have.

Self-study can certainly work for some people, but many students struggle with **motivation** from time to time. Having someone that they can lean on and talk to (whether it's about their lack of motivation or a particular language challenge) helps maintain interest in their study. It also helps create a sense of accountability. If you self-study, it's easy to find excuses for not putting in the work needed to reach a goal. Showing up in front of a teacher creates an emotional stake, where the student wants to show that they have 'done their homework'.

Interestingly, it seems that the more digital our world becomes, the more we crave **interaction** with others. Perhaps it's not surprising; human connection is vital for us as a species. Interacting with a language teacher is not only good for developing pronunciation and conversational skills. It also means having a human connection with someone who supports, cheers you on and motivates you. The way I see it, it's more like having a mentor, a guide and a fellow human being.

Today, we are literally drowning in information. We have access to so much information online at the click of a button that many find it overwhelming to sift through it all. Information is free and easily accessible, yet many people are time-poor and what they want most of all is help with how to implement techniques, rules and skills. This is where you as a teacher, and soon-to-be Language Teacher Rebel, come in.

What if I don't have an online presence?

You may think that it's too late to start teaching online. You might not have any social media channels set up. You might not have an email list. You see other teachers on social media platforms with large audiences, but you have never uploaded or posted to any platform, nor run an online live session. Is it too late? No. It's not too late. In fact, we are only just beginning to see the effects of the digital revolution.

Business expert Daniel Priestley argues that there's usually a time lag of 20–30 years before technology catches on. TV was invented in the 1930s, but it wasn't until the 1950s that it became more widely used. The first computers came out in the late 1960s, but it took until the 1980s before people started to buy computers for their home. Tim Berners-Lee invented the World Wide Web in 1989, but it took another 20 years before a significant number of people started to use it.

One in ten households in the UK, USA and the EU region did not have access to the internet at home in 2018–20, and only just over 50 per cent of the world's population currently has internet in their homes. In 1998, Google made the internet searchable. Social media emerged in 2004, and cloud computing in 2008. We are not yet seeing the full effects of search engines, social media and cloud computing. They will probably not be seen until at least 2030. So no, it's not too late. Far from it.

So how do you do it?

You might be wondering how you can become a Language Teacher Rebel. Do you need any particular training? Any specific work experience?

The answer is no.

All you need is a language that you can teach, an entrepreneurial mindset (or an interest in developing one), and a passion for helping people.

I come from Sweden. Although I was born in Stockholm, I grew up in rural Sweden, three hours outside of Stockholm. Before I started teaching, I only really had temporary jobs. I worked in over ten different areas, including working as a nanny, picking strawberries, helping set up a youth centre, as a supermarket cashier and as a family planning educator. I studied at university throughout most of my 20s, but not continuously.

My education and job experience are varied, to say the least. Throughout this time, I never really felt that I fit in. I always had an urge to develop, create and change things. It was like an itch that I was rarely allowed to scratch.

I took six months off after completing my bachelor's degree to 'go and see about a boy', so to speak. The problem was that he lived in New Zealand at the time. I managed to land a Swedish project-based job, working remotely. This was in 2003, and the internet connection was appalling, but it gave me the first taste of working remotely while travelling. The enormous sense of freedom of being in a different country while doing a job that I found interesting was worth a lot.

Six months later, my boyfriend and I ended up in the UK. I worked on a temporary basis for a year, but I yearned for freedom again and applied to do a PhD. However, as I got a better insight into the hierarchies of university departments, I began feeling it wasn't for me. Although I absolutely loved teaching and researching, I found it too restrictive and too fixed geographically. Would I have to apply for a position somewhere in a department, spend most days every week there, and only travel during holidays and for the odd conference?

Two years into my PhD in 2005, I needed a job so I could make some money. I tried my luck at a local betting shop, as I figured the hours were better than working in a pub. I only lasted two months.

A neighbour, who happened to be a German language teacher in a local school, casually said one day when I was complaining about the situation: 'Why don't you do something with your Swedish skills?' The thought had never crossed my mind. I lived in a medium-sized town in central England. Who would want to learn Swedish here?!

I found a website where language teachers could advertise their services, and I gave it a go. I got my very first student, a man living locally who was planning to move to Sweden in the future. I got a couple more students who lived about an hour from me but were happy to travel. I taught them in my house.

Then something happened. A man from Pennsylvania contacted me through the language-teaching website wanting lessons. He said he could phone me, so we started lessons over the phone. At the same time, Skype started to become more popular. I was already using it to contact friends and family in Sweden; what if I used Skype to teach students who didn't live near me? Could this be an opportunity? I started to suggest Skype in my adverts, and it took off.

In 2010, I had about 15 students a week, and I decided it was time to set up a website. A year later, I found an online booking system that I plugged in to my website and as of now I have taught over 20,000 hours online over 15 years. I have written a new version of *Teach Yourself Complete Swedish*. I have given talks at language conferences and I have been featured on BBC Two.

What I am trying to say is that your journey does not have to be straightforward. You may be a language teacher. You may have experience with sales, marketing and IT, you may not. You may just find yourself in a situation where you want to start something of your own, where you decide how you want to work. Where you can help people and share culture and language with others. All your past experience will be useful on your new Language Teacher Rebel journey. And you can learn the rest along the way.

A day in the life of a Language Teacher Rebel

So what's life like as a Language Teacher Rebel? Of course, it completely depends on you and how you design what suits you and your students best. Here is what my work-week looks like at the moment.

On Monday I usually have my first lesson at 7 a.m. I know this is quite early, but it's a good hour to offer, as it's 8 a.m. in Sweden and many students like having an hour of language learning before they start work. Because I am often at home, I usually get up at 6.30 a.m. Or sometimes even 6.45 a.m., if I am lazy. I get dressed in something comfortable and go to the kitchen and make myself a cup of tea. At 6.55 a.m. I glance at my booking system on the laptop in my office to see who has booked the first hour, and check their lesson log. This is where I wrote down what we did last lesson and what homework they have been given, so I can seamlessly begin the next lesson. I usually give two lessons, then have an hour's break at 9 a.m. I might do some yoga and have some breakfast. It's nice to have already worked two hours at this point, and also to get a break to stretch a bit and exercise.

I then teach again from 10 a.m. to 12 p.m. Afterwards I have a three-hour break until 3 p.m. where I cook food, watch TV or maybe go for a walk into town. In the summer, I often sit outside in the garden, listening to a podcast. I normally teach another two hours, followed by a free hour between 5 and 6 p.m. I round off the day with three more lessons in the evening, finishing at 9 p.m. If I'm fully booked, this is a long day, and I do the same on Tuesdays.

I have chosen this pattern for a reason. I have opted to compress my hours, so I often teach long hours on Mondays and Tuesdays. On Wednesdays, I start at 8 a.m. and finish at 7 p.m. and have a two- or three-hour lunch break. I then spend Thursdays and Fridays doing other projects, admin, or just taking some time off. In the past, I have also taught shorter days five days a week. But I have to admit, I really like how this pattern allows me to focus on my teaching during the first half of the week, and then have lots of freedom and flexibility on Thursdays and Fridays. I may or may not change my schedule in the future. The important thing is that I can choose how I want to work.

If you could choose your own hours, how would you prefer to design your days? When you have your own business, you can choose. You don't have to work 9–5 Monday to Friday unless you really want to. Would you teach five days a week? Or less? Would you teach during the day? Evenings? Would you teach in longer blocks, or would you space your lessons out? What else would you like to make time for? Family commitments? Exercise? Sleeping? Travelling? Art? Developing new projects? Reading?

Extreme flexibility

When you're a Language Teacher Rebel, you can set your own hours. You can also choose to move hours around. You might wonder how this works for the students. Won't they be expecting you to have the same hours available every week? Some do, but many don't. Flexibility is the reason they come to you for language lessons. Many will come because they can't attend a traditional language school. They might travel for work. They may live far away from a language school. They may work irregular hours, or work from home. They appreciate the flexibility that you offer, and the vast majority will have no problems with you shifting hours and days around occasionally.

I usually spend a month in California twice a year (because of my husband's work) and I continue to teach while I'm there. The time difference between Europe and California is 8–10 hours, so I teach afternoons and evenings (CET) during these periods. I would not be able to do this if I wasn't a Language Teacher Rebel. It would be impossible for me to have this level of flexibility if I was constrained to a classroom or a language school. Many students also find it interesting and it gives us even more to talk about.

A couple of times a year, I spend a week or two in Sweden with family. Again, being a Language Teacher Rebel allows me to take my work with me. Because I have chosen to work compressed hours, I can go to Sweden for a week and work Mondays to Wednesdays. I then have four days off with family and friends without having to take any time off. I can use the fact that I'm in Sweden during these lessons to show where I am staying. Some of my students have never been to Sweden, or rarely visit, so they love seeing the interior of a typical Swedish home. For me, it means a lot to stay connected to my native country and be able to work there. This would be extremely difficult to do if I had to teach in one particular physical location.

At home, my husband and I regularly board dogs. We are both obsessed with dogs, but because we travel regularly, we haven't had a dog of our own for a while. Because I work from home, we are able to board dogs that need looking after from time to time. As I am writing this, I am sitting on my sofa with a blanket over my legs, a cup of coffee next to me, and a brindle Mastiff-Staffy cross snoozing next to me. It's my idea of heaven.

The flexibility is more than simply geographical. When you become a Language Teacher Rebel, you also get to design and create. The creative flexibility and freedom you have means that you get to design your lesson plans and course curricula. You get to design visual content, social media posts and videos. You can dream up new products and services. You get to play with colours, fonts and photos. You can record and edit videos. You get to learn new things, about new pieces of software, new marketing ideas, new tools and tricks. You can do fun and silly things that make you laugh. You get to act on your creative ideas and focus on output and how to express yourself. This is also an extremely rewarding experience.

Reaching more people

Throughout my 15+ years as a Language Teacher Rebel, I have talked to doctors, nurses, midwives, authors, IT programmers, students, lecturers, managing directors, editors, archaeologists, solicitors, store managers, computer game designers, psychologists, priests, football coaches, sales people, HR people, marketing people, embassy workers, postmen, economists, bankers, musicians, film makers, translators, dancers, dog kennel owners, marine biologists, veterinary surgeons, post docs, PhD students, pharmacists, recruiters, entrepreneurs, unemployed people and more.

Due to the flexibility you have as a Language Teacher Rebel – especially if you do one-to-one sessions – you will be able to connect with your students in a deeper way than if you had taught them in a classroom setting. They will have their lessons while with their families, in-laws, or while at work. You will get a little window into their private world and learn a lot from them and about them. It's incredibly rewarding and fulfilling.

You also get an opportunity to make a difference in the world. Okay, it might sound cheesy and grandiose, but think about it. In our world today, we get exposed to different cultures. As people have travelled more during the past decades than ever before, things... happen. I met my husband while travelling in South East Asia. This led to me eventually moving from Sweden to the UK. Many of my students have met Swedish partners and started a new life in Sweden.

Close relationships with students

For me, a big part of the enjoyment of being a Language Teacher Rebel is the relationships you form with your students. It is indeed possible to form close relationships in classrooms too, especially if you're doing one-to-one teaching. However, dare I say that this fades into insignificance compared to the relationships you form when you teach online?

This might sound like a paradox, given that you're not in the same room as the student, but there's something about teaching online that enables you to get really close and personal with your students. I think it's a combination of the following factors: (1) the one-to-one environment, (2) the location, and (3) the online environment.

Firstly, when you teach one-to-one, you have an intense focus on your student and they will intensively focus on you. Of course, this can happen in a classroom too, and the effect will perhaps lessen if you teach a group online. Nevertheless, when you see a student for an hour once or twice a week, you may spend more time talking to them than they talk to their mum and dad. It might even be the same for you. I have taught some of my students regularly for over three years (the student I have taught the longest has been with me for conversation practice for over ten years), and I find that I think about them outside of the lessons. Whether it's a job interview, a house move, or even a difficult conversation at work, when something is happening in their lives, I am eager to find out. I sometimes miss them when they are on holiday, and I'm over the moon when a student who has taken a longer break returns to their lessons. I care deeply about them, not just as language students, but as people too, and I find it rewarding and humbling to be allowed to be a part of their lives.

Secondly, even though you may think you're 'only' teaching online, your students may have their lessons in their living room, their bedroom or their office. This can create a really intimate space, and you may catch glimpses of their everyday life in a way that you would never be able to do if they came to a classroom in a language school. I have had mums breastfeeding while speaking to me, I've had fathers soothing babies and children (and I have sometimes 'met' and spoken to their children), I have 'met' partners, work colleagues and pets. I have spoken to people while they have been travelling, from hotel rooms, or cafés, or just been out on a walk. I have 'gone with them' on holiday, so to speak. This creates a wonderful intimacy which I would thoroughly miss if I didn't teach online.

Thirdly, there's an interesting dynamic between the 'online distance' and the 'online closeness'. It leads to yet another level of depth in the relationship with a student. It's almost as if you, as an online teacher, represent a safe space where the student can talk about things that they wouldn't otherwise share with anyone. For example, I've had students tell me that they were planning to propose to their partner, or that they were pregnant, and no one else knew. I was considered 'safe', as I didn't know anyone in their circle. I wasn't a friend, colleague or family member who might accidently reveal what was about to happen. In their world, I only existed in their computer.

Some students have shared more difficult life situations with me for the same reason. I think speaking about something difficult in another language creates a certain perspective and emotional distance from which students have benefited.

In a sense, you end up being so much more than a language teacher. You're a friend and a confidant. And I truly believe that this kind of relationship is really valuable, especially if the student experiences a lack of motivation (which they all do occasionally, of course).

You may feel uncomfortable at the thought of this kind of intimacy with your students. Some may feel that there's a lack of hierarchy between the teacher and the student. In my 15+ years of experience, this is nothing to be afraid of. It's one of the most rewarding and deeply satisfying aspects of the whole Language Teacher Rebel lifestyle. And don't feel like you need to become some kind of counsellor or psychologist. Most of the time, it's just about connecting and listening to another human being.

The Language Teacher Rebel Mission

I mentioned earlier that you also get to make a difference in the world by being a Language Teacher Rebel. Let me explain what I mean by that.

Even though our world is becoming more connected and increasingly globalized, there's at least one area that is going in the opposite direction: the media. As a result of our personalized news feeds, cookies and other digital aids, a phenomenon called a 'filter bubble' has appeared. Eli Pariser coined this phrase in his 2011 TED talk where he describes his concern with web personalization. A filter bubble means that you can get different search results when googling something, compared to someone else, based on your previous search history.

A classic example is that people with a liberal political orientation who google 'BP' might get results about oil spills, but a person with a conservative leaning might get results that include investment information about the company. It's very easy these days to get a distorted view of our world through the internet and social media.

In a globalized world, many problems have become international and politicized: the environment, economics, social issues, etc. These global problems require global solutions, and for that we need global conversations. Teaching a language can support the development of global conversations. With the help of language, people can express themselves and share their thoughts with the world, especially with the aid of digital technologies.

Although not everyone wants to become a politician or an activist, I do feel that we as language teachers have a really important role to play in the future. As a Language Teacher Rebel, you can make a positive impact on the world. You can become a bridge-builder and make a difference.

You can expand people's 'bubbles' by teaching them a new language, so they can read and understand media and literature from a different country. You can also widen people's webs and networks by publishing, sharing and telling stories about that country and its culture. The internet and the digital era in which we now live give you amazing opportunities to reach people on an unprecedented global scale. But you'll also widen your own web and network and burst your own filter bubble through interacting with students from all over the world. It's a win-win.

Globalization today means that it's easier to get a job and move to a different country. It's easier to meet someone from a different country. But more dramatic events like climate change and conflicts will also force people to uproot and migrate to a different place. People will continue to move to other countries, for many reasons, and will need to absorb and integrate into a new culture. And those who are already in a country may wish to integrate further.

You can become a bridge between cultures and through your teaching you will pass this on to your students and make them bridges too. You will enable them to see different perspectives and enhance their cultural understanding. Culture is an important component to help people to connect, both regionally and globally. Familiarity overcomes and destroys fear. And in order to understand culture, language is a key component. Language skills are a ticket to participate in a culture. With digital tools, this journey can now start much earlier than before, and people can start to prepare before they even settle in a new country.

Since the 2020 outbreak of COVID-19, many traditional language schools have had to close, or try to move online. Many people are finding themselves at home for longer periods, perhaps with more time (and sometimes more money) on their hands, and they want to develop their skills further. Many students in Sweden have reached out to us to improve their Swedish, in case they need to look for a new job in the future.

The Digital Age has arrived, whether you like it or not. It's happening. And it has created a perfect environment for you as a language teacher to reach a much wider student base than has been remotely possible previously. You must develop a more entrepreneurial mindset and embrace change. You must become more curious, daring, and be ready to take on new challenges. By breaking free from the traditional 'classroom' way of thinking, you can make a living from home or from anywhere else, teaching people from all over the world.

From a more global perspective, you have an even bigger and more important opportunity as a Language Teacher Rebel. You can encourage integration on a worldwide scale. With your skills, together with technology, you can extend cultural values and understanding way beyond the classroom. You can build bridges, spread knowledge and increase empathy. And today, more than ever, that's badly needed.

Let's look into the future for a moment. What kind of lifestyle would you have as a Language Teacher Rebel? Would you set up a base at home but work with compressed hours, which would allow you more free time? Would you travel and teach at the same time? Would you have more time to spend with your family? What are the things that mean a lot to you, that you would be able to achieve if you were a Language Teacher Rebel with flexible work hours and work locations?

This is your rallying call.

Are you ready to become a Language Teacher Rebel?

If you are, let's go!

In the next chapter, we'll be looking into the importance of your mindset and how it's crucial for your success as a business owner. I highly recommend you read it, but if you want to dive straight into the details of developing products and services, jump ahead to Chapter 3.

Summary

- The Digital Age presents a huge number of opportunities for both language students and language teachers.

- It's not too late to start teaching online.

- Your varied experiences are your strengths.

- You will have a lot of flexibility as a Language Teacher Rebel. Think about how you would like to design your days and your work-week.

- Becoming a Language Teacher Rebel offers a mission to support integration and cultural understanding.

2

Mindset

When you start thinking about having your own business, you'll probably begin to worry about the technicalities. You may agonize over which website or booking system to use and how to find students online. Actually, those things are just practicalities. They are the 'what' part of setting up a business, and there are lots of practical solutions out there, as you will see in this book.

But, they are not the biggest hurdles you will face.

Your mindset is the one thing that can really stop you from achieving what you want. If you have never run your own business before, or never worked as a freelancer, one of the most important steps on your journey to becoming a Language Teacher Rebel is to improve your mindset.

Believe me, even as someone who has worked as a Language Teacher Rebel for over 15 years, I still work on my mindset all the time; it's a work in progress. And I have to, because it's so important for success and the ability to develop.

Your mindset is made up of all your beliefs that influence how you see yourself and the world around you. These could be beliefs you have inherited from your parents, from previous experiences, or from people and society around you. Belief statements often come together with words like 'because', 'will', 'won't', 'should' and 'shouldn't'. And sometimes (or quite often), these beliefs can stop us from achieving what we want.

Why you should focus on your mindset

The main reason you need to focus on mindset is that it's the only thing that can really hinder you. If you don't have the right mindset, if you don't trust yourself to make decisions for your business, if you don't feel confident about what you do and how you can help your students, or if you believe that you're not good with money, or that you shouldn't invest any money in your business because it's 'too risky', or that no one is interested in what you have to say, then it honestly doesn't matter which platforms or technology you use or how many digital marketing strategies you try to implement. Mindset is the game changer.

By working on your mindset, you will increase your trust and confidence in yourself. You will feel that you are good enough, that you are skilled and capable, that you have the confidence to show up in a space in front of others and know what you're talking about.

Another reason why you should be focusing on mindset is that it truly influences how you see the world. There are some fascinating scientific facts that I'd like to share with you, that blow my mind every time I think about them.

Consider all the senses we have: taste, hearing, smell, sight and touch. All of our senses are constantly processing information from the world around us. Apparently, there are approximately 2 million pieces of information around us at any given moment. Two million! Of course, we can't process all of that information. That would be impossible. Instead, our brain processes just over 120 pieces of information at a time. Our brain uses filters based on what it believes we think is important. This happens without us even realizing it; it's not a conscious decision. Our brain filters down even further to between **five and seven** pieces of information to actually focus on. So, we only pay attention to five to seven things at any one time.

The filters that our brain uses depend on many different things, including time, location, language, memories, mood, decisions, values, beliefs and identity. These filter everything we see and experience. So, for example, how we feel and what we believe will impact how we see the world around us. In this instance, your brain will prefer information that agrees with your beliefs or mood, because your brain wants to prove you correct. If you believe that you're not capable of making business decisions for yourself, the evidence you'll be presented with (automatically, without realizing or controlling it) will support that belief.

There are many things you can do to work on your mindset, but here are some specific ideas to combat *limiting beliefs* that will help you as you transition to becoming a Language Teacher Rebel.

Challenge limiting beliefs

Firstly, you need to start recognizing what your beliefs are. This can be tricky at first, as we're often not even aware of our own beliefs. But you can start by reflecting on a couple of areas that are important if you are going to run your own business: money and work.

BELIEFS ABOUT MONEY

How do you look at money? Is it the root of all evil? Is it important? Is it there to be spent? Do you feel you are good with money? Do you feel you have to work hard to become wealthy? Is it selfish to want to become rich? Do you believe that you can earn a lot of money doing what you love?

Now, fill in the blanks:

Money is _____.

Money for me means _____.

Then ask yourself the following questions:

1. Is this belief serving me right now?

2. What would be a more helpful belief?

3. What evidence is there to support this new belief? (Look around, and you'll find lots of good examples that support this new belief.)

BELIEFS ABOUT WORK

There are three main categories of limiting beliefs about work.

- Beliefs about yourself *(I'm too introverted / I'm not smart enough / I never succeed)*

- Beliefs about other people *(Nobody's interested in X / People aren't naturally supportive / They'll think I'm crazy)*

- Beliefs about the way the world is organized *(You can't become successful if you don't have connections / You have to have at least X years' worth of savings to make a leap / The 'system' is set up to make it hard)*

Go through these three categories and try to get a sense of what your honest beliefs are. And don't feel ashamed if you realize that you have beliefs that you don't like. This is a part of the process.

Once you have clarified current beliefs, ask yourself the same questions as you did when you looked at beliefs about money:

1. Is this belief serving me right now?

2. What would be a more helpful belief?

3. What evidence is there to support this new belief?

FIVE COMMON LIMITING BELIEFS

Here are five very common limiting beliefs and how you can challenge them.

Remember these when you start teaching online, as your students will most likely struggle with some of the same limiting beliefs in their language-learning process!

1. 'It's hopeless'

Fill in the blank: 'I'll never be able to start/make a living out of teaching online, because _____.'

The problem with this belief is that if you think something isn't possible, you won't even try to do it.

You can easily challenge this belief by, instead of thinking that it's hopeless, asking 'How is it possible?'

2. 'I'm helpless'

An example could be that you think you'll never be able to run your own online language-teaching business, because no one has taught you how. When you don't know how to do something or think a goal is too ambitious, you start to feel helpless about your situation. The weight of the task or the steps involved seem too difficult, and you give up before you begin.

Ask yourself instead: 'What do I already know about it?' and 'What can I do to learn more?'

3. It's useless

You might think that it's too late to start teaching online, or that you shouldn't bother learning about it, as it will take too much time before you see results. If something doesn't seem achievable, you may view it as useless. But most events have both short-term and long-term results. If you only focus on short-term results you can miss an opportunity.

Ask yourself instead: 'How is it achievable?'

4. I'm blameless

With this belief, you'll blame someone else or some external factor for why you can't do what you want to. For example, 'I can't start my own business, because the economy is so bad at the moment and it would be a risk.'

To be honest, blaming external events or situations is the easy and lazy way out. Interestingly though, once the current external event is over (the economic situation improves, for example), you'll quickly find something else to blame for your situation.

Ask yourself instead: 'How am I responsible?'

5. I'm not good enough

'I can't run my own online business, because I'm not smart/techy/business-minded/entrepreneurial enough.'

Feeling worthless and undeserving puts the blinders on you. You fail to notice what you're good at and consequently think you're not good enough.

Ask yourself instead: 'How do I deserve it?'

When you address and challenge your beliefs, it can feel scary at first. You are basically rocking the foundations of a belief system that you may have had for a long time. However, when you choose to change a belief, the effect can be both immediate and dramatic.

You can actually choose to just believe something else. It's your choice!

The more you look around for evidence for your new belief, the more examples you will find, which will help to build your confidence in your new belief system.

FEAR OF FAILURE

When you start thinking about setting up your own online language-teaching business, you will probably experience fear of failure. This is normal and natural, but it can be very limiting and if you let it fester, it can stop you from achieving what you want.

A common fear is the fear of making the wrong choice. 'What if I choose the wrong name/logo/website for my business?', 'What if I choose the wrong social media channel for my marketing?', 'What if I choose the wrong product or niche?'

Firstly, let me tell you this: there is no such thing as the wrong choice. This might sound clichéd, but it's actually true. There are only different choices with different consequences. The beauty of being a Language Teacher Rebel is that you get to decide what is right for you, as you define what success is for you. No one else does. And if you make a choice that you would like to amend or adjust, you just change it. It's as simple as that. I have lost count of how many times I have changed, amended and tweaked things in my business. It doesn't matter.

Fear of failure can lead to failure to take action. You feel you don't know enough and you need someone to tell you what to do. You need to read just one more book or listen to just one more podcast. It can lead you to spending months and months on planning and researching, but not actually creating anything.

When you are planning, it feels like you are being productive, but actually you are not. Planning is good, but you should spend the majority of your time taking action, not planning to take action. This kind of planning is sometimes called 'procrasti-planning' (such a great word!). I have suffered quite a lot from it and I am still working on reducing it. Try to spend at least 75 per cent of your time taking action and be careful not to spend too much time planning. And stop making excuses.

Another common fear is that you are not going to make enough money, or not get enough students. But for this to even be a consideration, you need to work out what 'enough' means. How much money (per week/month/year)? How many students? And what time frame are we talking about?

Most people think in terms of all or nothing; they think they will make absolutely nothing at all (overly pessimistic), or they think they will be swimming in money in no time (overly optimistic).

The truth, as always, lies somewhere in-between. It's definitely possible to set up a language-teaching business online and learn techniques, including marketing and sales, that will help you achieve that goal – it's just that it will take both time and hard work. Unfortunately, a lot of people just aren't willing to put the effort in and won't have the patience to wait for those results.

IMPOSTER SYNDROME

Another common fear-related experience that many new business owners have is imposter syndrome. This is the feeling that you're not good enough, not enough of an expert, and that you're faking it. If you experience imposter syndrome (which most people do), then there are a couple of things you can do to overcome it.

Surround yourself with other people who are on the same journey as you. Find your tribe. Look for online groups and communities where other people are working towards the same goal. Go to entrepreneur meetups and networking events so you can share your experiences and find supportive people to surround yourself with. I am not saying you have to change your friends, but it's good to broaden your circle to include other people in the same situation (especially if your friends work in more traditional industries). Also, surround yourself with other people who can help you, be it mentors, business coaches, or generally inspiring people.

You should also take a look at how you define success and get very clear on what your own intentions are and why you want to do this. The more clarity and conviction you have for your vision of your business and your life overall, the less you'll look to other people for validation and guidance on what you should be doing.

Build your confidence and develop your intuition

As Language Teacher Rebels, we need to nurture our entrepreneurial mindset. We need to build our confidence and develop our intuition, in order to be able to take the steps we need to grow. Here are four things you can do straight away.

TUNE OUT FROM THE NEWS

I'll admit it: I'm a news junkie. In the past, I automatically checked the news headlines several times a day, sometimes even several times an hour. I identify as a curious person who likes to learn and know what's going on in the world, and being on top of the news was a part of that.

But the problem is that when I check the news, it often sets me off on a spiral of associations in my mind. I read something about local politics, which reminds me of something else that I just *have to* look up. Or it brings up something that I was unaware of, that I just *have to* look up and learn about.

The other problem is that news (especially online news) is designed to keep your attention for as long as possible. News outlets know that they can engage people if they can stir their emotions: outrage, curiosity, anger, surprise, relief, and all those other rollercoaster emotions. And to be honest, it's draining! Sometimes it can even be downright depressing. It drains your energy and keeps your mind occupied with other things, instead of thinking about your business and your long-term plans.

So, cut down on media consumption for a while, just to give yourself a break and create some productive space.

Take responsibility for what you consume. If something big happens that you need to know about, you can be sure you'll hear it from other people around you.

STOP SPENDING TIME WITH/ON PEOPLE WHO GET YOU DOWN

If everyone around you inspires you, great! You can skip this step. If you do have some people around you who can get you down, you don't have to stop seeing them altogether, but try and surround yourself with people who inspire you. This can be in person, but also people that you follow online.

People you follow or have conversations with online will have an influence on you. Even if you don't know them and will never talk to or meet them in person. Things they say and write will influence what ideas you think about and what you think is possible to achieve. Take some time to carefully go through who you spend time with and also who you follow online (both personal friends and people you don't know).

IMPERFECT ACTION

Ever thought of something you'd like to try, and then immediately been swamped with thoughts that begin like this: 'What if...?', 'What will happen...?', 'What if I can't/won't...?', 'How would I...?' When beginning a new project, I sometimes used to start thinking about potential problems that were eight or ten steps down the line. Before I'd even started! And I still sometimes get stuck in this way of thinking.

The thing with having an entrepreneurial mindset is that we *have to* get comfortable with taking steps without knowing exactly where they will lead. You won't be able to know the end result at the beginning of the journey. But the most important thing is that you do something. You need to take action.

One thing you should do immediately is to practise taking **imperfect action**. Things you do won't be perfect; they can't be. Instead, take the minimum viable action to get your ideas off the ground. Set up ONE social media account (not five) where you start posting content about what you do. You might start without a booking system, but you can still teach online. Or you may start with a booking system, but not set up a website. One minimal viable action is to set up a video-conferencing platform like Skype or Zoom, for example, and you can teach online.

Recently, I really wanted to try and launch a self-paced online course. I listened to lots of podcasts talking about huge courses that they priced at over $1,000 per student. I had never tried the systems they used, never run a professional webinar, and the whole thing seemed overwhelming. I decided to take minimal viable action instead and set up a small course on a topic that I was used to teaching and that I knew people were struggling with.

From start to finish, it took me less than 30 days: approximately two weeks to create the content for the course, and about two weeks to market and launch it. I used a simple set up and things I already had and knew. During five days of selling, I sold the course to 25 people. I know it's not earth-shattering, but I was so chuffed that 25 people actually bought it! And now I have a course that I can sell again, and it will become even more profitable every time I sell it (as I don't have to create the course content again).

When you take action, you will start to trust yourself, and trust that you can take action. You don't need other people's permission to do so.

A good way to nurture your intuition is to follow your curiosity. If you struggle to do this in your business, start with something outside of your business. Read an unrelated book about a subject that you are curious about. Start a hobby that you think you would enjoy, or take up an old hobby you used to love. Start listening to your body and take action on it. If your body tells you that you need some rest, make time for some rest. By doing so, you will train yourself to listen inwards and follow your gut instincts.

Also, realize that there are no mistakes to be made. There are no wrong blog posts to publish, no wrong subject headlines in emails, no wrong lesson designs. These are all just decisions to make; pick something, go with it, put it out there and see what happens. And learn from it.

OVERCOMING OBJECTIONS FROM OTHERS

Although a lot of mindset thinking is personal, you may also come up against other people's mindsets. When you decide to start something new, people around you may object. They may discourage you and say things that make you doubt your ideas. So how can you overcome objections from others?

It's not about you

The first thing you need to realize is that most likely it's not about you, it's about them. They are expressing their own fears and worries. It's in no way a reflection of what you're capable of.

If they are people that you're not close to (colleagues, acquaintances, distant family members), you can just ignore them. They don't know you well, and it doesn't really matter what they think. If they are people closer to you, you should know that they probably don't mean to hurt you. They care about you and want what's best for you. They're just expressing their own fears and mindsets.

Protect yourself

If you're at the earlier stages of your journey to becoming a Language Teacher Rebel, I would recommend you try to protect yourself to start with. You don't have to share your early thoughts and ideas with everyone.

When you start thinking about these steps, you're likely to have lots of ideas that might change along the way. This is a completely natural part of the journey, and you need to allow it to run its course. But if you share every twist and turn with everyone (especially those who might be a bit sceptical), they could see you as unfocused and undecided. This will only make their worries worse.

Therefore, it's better if you keep some of the earlier stages to yourself, or only share them with people who you know will be supportive of your intentions and dreams. Later, when you have a clearer picture of what things will look like, you can share your ideas with others too.

Find your tribe

As at so many stages on this journey, finding your tribe is really important. Surrounding yourself with people who are on the same journey as you is both inspiring and comforting. You'll be able to relate to each other, inspire each other, share new ideas and cheer each other on. If you want to join our Language Teacher Rebel Tribe, go to annelihaake.com.

Summary

- Working on your mindset is one of the most important things to do as you become a business owner.

- Explore your mindset continuously, especially around work and money, with a non-judgmental and accepting attitude.

- Surround yourself with people who inspire you.

- Get to know your common fears so you can recognize when they visit you.

- Take steps to build your confidence and develop your intuition.

3

Plan and design your products

What can you offer as a Language Teacher Rebel? In this chapter, I'll go through different types of services and products that you can use in your online business. I'll also discuss how to price your offers and how you can start to create a neat Product Ecosystem, where your products in this system all support each other.

In order to stand out as a Language Teacher Rebel, you need to find your niche, which will be discussed in the next chapter. But first, let's start by talking about different types of services and products so you can get an idea of the things you can do.

Your offer

When you look at successful businesses, you'll see that they all offer their clients a 'new opportunity'. When Apple released the iPod, they didn't just make a moderately better CD- or MP3-player with more space. They created a new opportunity where a person could carry around their whole music library in their pocket. When Uber started working on their app in 2009, they didn't just improve on taxi booking services available at the time. They introduced dynamic pricing that fluctuates based on supply and demand, cashless payments, a 'one-tap' booking system, and an app that allows the driver to see exactly where the customer is (and vice versa). You can spot this pattern of a new opportunity offer in all innovative areas: technology, sports, health, travelling, business, even in religion.

Look at it like this: your goal is not to improve something in your industry. Your goal is instead to *replace what is not working with something better.*

You might start looking at what other language teachers are currently doing, and think that you could do the same thing, but just a bit better. When you do that, you're not offering your students a new opportunity. You're offering them an 'improvement offer'. The entrepreneur Russell Brunson says that the issue with improvement offers is that they are much more difficult to sell.

One reason for this is that people are usually more sceptical of improvement offers, because they would have to acknowledge that whatever they tried before didn't work for them. Or, to be more precise, that they have failed. I am not saying they have failed, but they probably feel this way, consciously or subconsciously. No one wants to feel like they have failed.

Another reason is that they will also be reminded about the pain and the struggles associated with their past failure. But they don't know the process of a new opportunity, so they will be much more likely to try it out. Yet another reason is that when you try to make an improvement offer, you're competing against other providers of the same thing in the same niche. This can quickly lead to a battle for lower prices (and a race to the bottom).

So how can you deliver your offer? Let's look at some options for delivering language lessons online.

Services and products

In this section we'll look more specifically into each of the commonly used methods of delivering online language tuition, and we'll also explore how they compare in categories like cost, time, resources, tech skills and scalability (on a scale of high to low).

ONE-TO-ONE (LIVE)

One-to-one (live) is a lesson in real time with one student, delivered through video-conferencing platforms such as Skype, Teams or Zoom. You sit in front of your computer for a set amount of time and speak directly to your student.

Expense/cost: low

The cost of delivering a one-to-one lesson is very low. Many video communication platforms are free (or have free plans), and as long as you have a laptop, broadband and material to use, you can deliver a lesson easily. You may want to set up a booking system to make it easier for you to manage (more on how to do this later).

Time: low

If you set up a digital library with teaching materials, you shouldn't have to spend much time preparing your lesson. You will practise speaking with your students, go through homework, introduce and explain new learning modules and set new homework.

Resources/tools: low

Your teaching material, which may require some initial organizing, will be on your laptop and you'll use certain online tools (video conferencing, payment tools, etc.), but it doesn't require a lot of resources to get up and running.

Tech skills: low

If you have never used video conferencing, you will need a small amount of time to get used to it, but this method of delivery requires comparatively low levels of tech skills.

Scalability: low

Here's the downside of teaching live. You can't really scale this type of teaching beyond the number of hours you're prepared to teach. You're simply selling your time. However, you will get loads of useful feedback on what you do, which can generate ideas for other products that you could design in the future. So if you're just starting out, this is an excellent way to get hours under your belt and get used to working online.

GROUP (LIVE)

Live group sessions are group lessons that you teach online. The format is pretty much the same as for one-to-one, but you'll have more than one person in your session. Again, you'll sit in front of your computer and teach for a set amount of time. Or you could, for example, run an online language café/conversation practice session.

Expense/cost: low

This has pretty much the same costs as for one-to-one, which are almost none. Many video-conferencing platforms offer free accounts for one-to-one calls and sometimes also for group calls.

Time: low

Again, this is very similar to one-to-one live sessions as you'll be teaching live and you'll have your digital teaching library set up.

Resources/tools: low

As it's the same type of delivery method, your resources will be the same as for one-to-one teaching. Sometimes teachers who teach group lessons mention that it can be a little difficult if any of the participants have connection problems or sit in a noisy environment. This will obviously affect the rest of the group, whereas when you teach one-to-one it's not so much of an issue. But as you can often mute all participants, this can be easily overcome.

Tech skills: medium

Because you'll be connecting more people into one call, there are a few more things to think about (and a few more things that can go wrong). However, it's quite easy to do a couple of test runs with some friends, to make sure you feel comfortable with the format before you start professionally.

Scalability: medium

With group lessons, you can take on more students for the time you're teaching, which means a higher hourly income for you.

ONLINE COURSES

An online course can be delivered in many different ways, but it's usually a pre-recorded video course with accompanying exercises. The course could be videos of you talking into the camera, and recorded slideshows. This means that you will not teach live, but the student will go through the course at their own pace. The course could have little or no contact with you as a teacher (100 per cent self-study), or it could

involve sending in certain assignments for you to correct
and give feedback on (written assignments, or video snippets
of their speaking practice, for example). It could also be a
membership/subscription service, where you give access to
your training materials (video tutorials and workbooks, for
example) at a specific cost for a set amount of time (think of
it like a gym membership).

Expense/cost: medium

A good online course will require a higher financial
investment than teaching live. For it to be of decent quality,
you may need to invest in some equipment beyond your
laptop and your phone (such as an editing program). It
doesn't have to be super-fancy though, and I have created
some online courses with just my laptop. If you choose to
host your course on a platform (like Udemy, SkillShare,
Thinkific or Teachable, for example), there can be costs
involved there too.

Time: high first, then medium

This method of teaching is very much a case of producing
first and then letting the course work for you. I wouldn't view
this as passive income once you start selling your course, as
you need to work on marketing when you launch the course
(and before you launch too). And you may want to offer your
students some kind of community where you can help and
support them (for example, a private group on a social media
platform), which requires time too. Most of the time is spent
designing and launching the course, with some further time
required after launch. The idea is to create the course and
then sell it repeatedly (perhaps with some minor updates). The
more times you sell the course, the more profitable it becomes.

Resources/tools: medium

As mentioned under expense/cost, online courses will require more tools than live lessons, such as video-editing software, course platforms and email list programs. (There is more on email list programs in Chapter 6.)

Tech skills: medium

The main tech skills required for creating online courses (that you don't need when teaching live) are recording and editing video.

Scalability: high

Because it's an online course, the scalability is very high. You sell the course or access to the material, not your time, so you can accept as many students as you like.

BLENDED COURSES

A blended course could, for example, be an online course that also includes a couple of live sessions (one-to-one or group sessions) in the price, or perhaps a live webinar. This will require some extra time be set aside to do the live sessions, but otherwise the criteria are quite similar to the online courses.

OTHER PRODUCTS

There are many other products that you can create and sell online to complement your online business. You can sell recordings, videos on particular topics (like a masterclass) and books. You can also create exercises or worksheets and sell them too.

For someone who is just starting out, I would say that the easiest way is to begin with one-to-one live sessions, but with a view to creating other offers further down the line. When you begin with one-to-one sessions, you can refine your online teaching methods and also gather reviews and feedback, which you can later use as social proof (showing that other people like what you offer) for selling your other products.

How to productize a service

Package, package, package! When you're selling lessons online, it's all about packaging. One easy way to sell live lessons (and one that I have used successfully for quite a long time) is to bundle lessons into discount packages: 10 for x amount of money, or 25 for x amount of money.

However, an even better offer is if you package your service into smaller, actionable chunks – once you have found your niche (more on that in the next chapter) and thought about what it is that you'll help your students with. For example, if you want to help introverted and nervous speakers, create a package that helps them overcome a specific problem, such as 'How to buy a cup of coffee/have a phone conversation/talk socially for ten minutes with confidence.'

Make small and actionable steps to help your students overcome their problem. It's much better to help with something relatively small and specific (or what might look like a small thing to you but could be huge for your student) and have them succeed, rather than get stuck on a long, never-ending marathon course. Or there could be a particular area of the language's grammar that often causes people problems. For example, in Swedish, people struggle with possessive reflexive pronouns. A small, actionable package on how to understand and use Swedish possessive reflexive pronouns would literally fly off the shelf!

Add actionable content to your course. This could be included as homework, worksheets, exercises, and tips on how to apply it in real life. Also, design a tracker (for example, a PDF file that you give to students), or encourage students to record videos continuously, so they can track their progress, and go back to see how far they have come.

Come up with some fun names for your packages. Don't be boring. A package on Spanish verbs doesn't have to be called 'Spanish Verbs 1'. Use some fun and inspiring words; even 'Spanish Verb Specialist' is better than just 'Spanish Verbs'. Or use something from your language that would fit nicely, and add a subtitle explaining what it is.

How to price

There is a myth that online teaching is worth less than traditional classroom teaching. Let me say straight away that I don't believe this at all! One of the reasons given is that online teachers do not have to pay room/building costs or hire, as they work from home. While this is true, you're not just charging for the actual time you spend teaching. You're also marketing yourself (just as traditional language schools do) and you're creating a very convenient environment for your students, who don't have to spend time and money on travelling to a particular location.

If you find this way of seeing it challenging, think about when you do something else for the sake of convenience. If you order food delivery to your home, you pay extra for that, right? By offering online tuition, you're saving time for your students; time that they can spend doing something else (for example, making more money or spending time somewhere else). Or you're enabling them to do something they couldn't otherwise do, maybe because they can't travel to a traditional language school, etc.

In addition, you're doing many other things than just teaching when running an online business. You might invest in some equipment to make the lesson experience better. You may invest in a course on something that will help you develop your skills as an online language teacher. You'll spend time creating teaching materials, or content for marketing yourself to the world.

Interestingly, people often produce better results when they have invested money in something. Think about it; if you go to a free event, you may find it interesting and inspiring. But if you have paid out of your own pocket for a course, you're going to make sure you get the absolute most out of it. You're much more likely to 'do your homework', so to speak. When people pay, they pay attention. This is why a lower price does not automatically mean better. Your pricing also speaks of how you value yourself. If you set your pricing at the bottom of the market, it will appear that you don't have a lot to offer. You will seem cheap, and not in a good way. Don't enter that race to the bottom.

When you teach live, you will to some extent be tied down to an hourly rate, whereas when you sell online courses and blended courses, you're a bit freer to set your cost per course. But, if you have created a new opportunity, you can take a higher hourly 'live' rate than other teachers in your niche. Why? Because your product is different, so it can't really be compared to other products in the same way as if you're just another Italian/Spanish/English teacher online.

Instead of thinking about what you should charge, think about why you should charge what you do. This forces you to switch the perspective to that of your student and justify what you're actually giving them. You're not just giving them your expertise in conjugating verbs, for example. You're giving them the ability to speak to their in-laws, get a new job in a new country, interact socially in their new language and so on. You're doing so much more than just teaching one specific thing.

CALCULATING AN HOURLY RATE

If you absolutely need to calculate your hourly rate, you could look at the average salary of language teachers in your country. Look online for the specific type of language teacher salaries (ESL/TEFL/modern languages, etc.). For example, let's imagine that the average salary is 30,000 GBP per year before tax. On top of this, you need to add an amount to cover the cost of your business (overheads). As you'll be working from home, your overheads will be a bit lower than for someone who needs to rent an office. Examples here are given in £ so remember to convert to the appropriate currency for you.

You can add 25 per cent to your cost (typical overhead figures are between 25 and 40 per cent), which means you'll need to get a total of £37,500 in from your students per year.

£30,000 + 25% = £37,500

Let's say you want this income to come from teaching students one-to-one, and you could realistically handle 25 lesson hours a week (the rest of the week you have flexibility to work on creating content, marketing and other admin, or just take some time off if you need to). If you want to factor in, say, five weeks of holiday, calculate 47 weeks of work.

25 hours x 47 weeks = 1,175 hours per year

Then, just divide £37,500 by the number of hours per year:

£37,500 / 1,175 = £32 per hour per student

If you were planning to run group lessons, you would probably charge less per student (since people expect to pay less for groups as they won't get as much attention from the teacher as they would in a one-to-one lesson). These lessons may take a little longer to prepare, as you may need to create exercises suited for the group, unless they are all at the exact same level.

BUT (and this is a big but) if you are (which you should be) offering something new and unique, and you're creating your own niche, then you can charge more. Remember, this example is only comparing the price to the salary of a language teacher who's probably teaching in a classroom environment in a language school. If you have spent time figuring out your niche, and you're providing a solution that your students want in a new and creative way, then you should **definitely** charge more than the equivalent 'average language teacher' salary.

CALCULATING A PRICE FOR A BLENDED COURSE

Another way to work out a price, especially for a blended course, is to think about how many students you want to work with per week. How many students could you realistically look after per week? If you wanted to create a service that also includes other tailor-made features (perhaps individually recorded glossaries, or feedback on written texts outside of your meetings with your students), how many students could you have?

Just as an example, let's say that you decide you could have 20 students per week, and your service is a package that takes students two months to complete. Let's say you could run this course four times per year, realistically. If you want this to be your only income, you would need to sell 80 enrolments per year.

Then think about what you need to live comfortably per year. Let's say, for argument's sake, that you would feel comfortable with £40,000 per year pre-tax. To make this amount of money by selling the package to 80 students, you need to price the course at somewhere around £500. And you need to sell it to 80 people per year, in order to hit your revenue goal.

Your next step in this example would be to start with the idea of a £500 course that would be 6–8 weeks long, and begin planning the design. How many hours of one-to-one calls per student would be required? What else would the package include (for example, tailor-made resources, e-books, recordings, a private online community available to students, written feedback, etc.)?

This is just an example. You might opt for more students and offer group-coaching calls instead of one-to-one calls. Or you could add different tiers to your offer. Basic tier (the cheapest) is just the course (with no interaction with you), next tier (a bit more expensive) is access to group calls for a period of time, and the premium tier (most expensive) could also include a couple of one-to-one sessions with you. Or you might decide on a different amount that you would like to achieve financially. This is a different way of thinking about price, instead of being restricted by the average salary as a benchmark.

Creating a Product Ecosystem

A Product Ecosystem is a proven way to design different types of products that will work together in a system. An ecosystem. One example of this is Daniel Priestley's ATM (Ascending Transaction Model), which includes four products: 1) a First Free Offer, 2) an Intro Product, 3) a Core Product and 4) a Product for Clients.

When you're thinking about the products that you'll start to design as a Language Teacher Rebel, you should also start to design a Product Ecosystem. This is not something that you'll complete in a week or two, but I want to introduce you to the idea now, so you have a longer-term plan and a broader perspective on how your offers can work together in the future.

Don't feel like you need to create the whole ecosystem immediately; you can start with one or two products. But keep in mind that this is what you ultimately want to strive for.

FIRST FREE OFFER

A free offer is exactly that. It's free. It's something that you'll offer free of charge to show your students what you can do. If you look at the most successful businesses, you'll find that they all have one of these free offers. Apple offers iTunes for free, mobile apps usually have a free version that you can try, and so on.

Ideally, a free offer should be something that your students can download; in other words, a digital product. I don't recommend offering free live lessons (some call it a 'demo/trial lesson') as a First Free Offer. Some people advocate this, but I don't think it's a good idea. Why? Because it's not something that your students can keep. They can't keep coming back to it, or look at it again. Nor can they share it with others. A trial lesson only exists while you're teaching it. Also, you have to give your time for free again and again and again. When you create a free digital product, you create it once and then it does the work for you. People can download it as much as they want, without it taking any more of your time.

What kind of digital products could you create? You could create a short and specific e-book about your topic. You could create a webinar that you pre-record and offer access to for free. You could also create a brief email course for free. You can set up email courses for free in an email list system (more on this in Chapter 7), where people sign up and get an email per day for a short time (between five and seven days). This could include written content, video tutorials or audio tutorials. One good thing about email courses is that you actually train your prospective students to open your emails! This is good for when you want to reach out to them at a later stage with other offers.

Your First Free Offer should solve a very specific problem in your niche. It should give your students a real sense of achievement and build trust in you that you can help them overcome a particular problem that they have. Because it's free, the leap they have to take to get it will be small. You'll have a chance to 'show off' and let them get to know you. This will build awareness of you and your brand, which will make them more likely to engage with you and eventually spend money on your paid products. It's a 'try before you buy' kind of approach. It's also a really good way to allow people to share your work with others, which means your free product will spread further and reach more people.

A First Free Offer is often called a Lead Magnet, and is discussed in more detail in Chapter 7.

INTRO PRODUCT

Your Intro Product is the next step in your Product Ecosystem. This is a small product that you'll sell at an affordable price. And when I say affordable, I mean probably no more than what a meal would cost. The offer could be either the next logical step following your First Free Offer, a complement to it, or a more in-depth version of it. If someone shows an interest in your First Free Offer, it makes sense to take the next step and buy your Intro Product.

This is why it has to be logical in some way (next step, complement, or more in-depth). If you create a First Free Offer about one thing, and then create an Intro Product about something completely different, it won't make sense to your students. Why would they buy your Intro Product, when they were initially drawn to you because of your First Free Product?

Another way you can design your Intro Product, which works very well, is as a means to share your ideas. Not general ideas, not old ideas, but your own unique ideas. In the world we live in today, information is cheap and easy to come by, compared to 30 years ago. You can sell your ideas cheaply, and then focus on making money by helping your students to *implement* those ideas. I'm sure you can relate to the feeling of being overwhelmed with information. There's just so much of it available online, often free of charge. People these days are more interested in getting help to implement it. Therefore, you can use an Intro Product as a way to define your own unique ideas, so that people can get to know you and become inspired to work with you to implement these ideas.

Like your First Free Offer, your Intro Product could be a digital product (a downloadable e-book, a set of short video tutorials, audio files, etc.) or a physical book. It could also be a webinar or a group session that you teach live. Make sure you get people's email addresses when they buy your Intro Product.

CORE PRODUCT

Your Core Product is the heart of your online business; this is what you'll become known for and what will make you money. If you teach live, this product will be your lessons. If you create an online course, your course will be your Core

Product. You'll solve people's problems, or create a significant benefit to them with your Core Product. Your First Free Offer and Intro Product will give people a taste of how easily you can solve problems for them, but with your Core Product you'll do it fully and thoroughly. This product has to be a real solution to your customers' problems in your area of expertise.

For your Core Product to be a real solution, it should focus on implementation. This means it should focus on the 'how to', rather than 'why'. This means that you'll help people to make a change that they haven't been able to accomplish alone. You can either work with them to implement it properly (for example, through live teaching or as a coach), or you can offer a path or methodology together with appropriate tools and exercises so that they can implement it on their own (in an online course, for example). This will save them lots of time, and that's what many people are prepared to pay for.

Your Core Product will be priced to be profitable and should be so good that people can't stop talking about it (and can't help telling their friends how good it is). You should never lose money on this product or undersell it. Through your Core Product, you'll get paid fairly for what you do. You'll do this by designing a special methodology that really works in your own niche. You'll also need to design nice-looking content online and a professional-looking website for your Core Product, and you'll position yourself as an expert within this specific niche.

PRODUCT FOR CLIENTS

Eventually, you may also want to consider creating what is known as a Product for Clients. This is the logical next step for clients who have bought your Core Product and want more. They were very pleased with your Core Product, and they want to know what the next step is. Of course, if you teach live (one-to-one or group sessions) you may have repeat students. If you have a business model where people go from absolute beginner to intermediate, and so on, they will keep coming back for more to take them through to the next level. But if you have a specific focus, you may be able to offer your 'graduates' something else.

Comparing this to some other industries might make it clearer. Let's say a Personal Trainer has a programme focused on weight loss. When their students have worked through their programme, they have (hopefully) lost some weight. A potential Product for Clients (and a very logical next step) is to offer a style consultant service, as the students may want to buy some new clothes that will fit their new body. This could be set up in collaboration with someone else. Or a car seller may offer their customers yearly maintenance or repairs. You get the idea. As a Language Teacher Rebel, you need to think about what the logical next step could be for your students. Once they have mastered what it is you sell as your Core Product, what is the next step for them?

Once you have developed your own Product Ecosystem, you'll find that all the parts in the system support each other and work together seamlessly. But be patient; this takes more than a couple of months to develop. Rome wasn't built in a day, as they say.

Summary

- Create a new opportunity, not an improvement offer.

- Choose a service or product that you want to create, based on how they compare in the different categories, and package it nicely.

- Teaching live one-to-one is the easiest way to start.

- Remember that 'online' doesn't mean a low price.

- Aim to eventually create a Product Ecosystem, including:

  - a First Free Offer
  - an Intro Product
  - a Core Product
  - a Product for Clients.

4

Finding your micro-niche

Can you be successful as an online English teacher or an online Spanish teacher? Could you market yourself online in a way that attracts new students? Yes, of course you can.

But here's the thing: unless you teach a particularly rare language that no one else teaches (perhaps Indonesian Liki or Ethiopian Ongota), the chances are that there are other language teachers who teach the same language. In other words, you will have competitors. This means you need to try and stand out. Simply listing the number of hours you have taught, or the fact that you may have a teaching degree, will just look dull.

I am a Swedish teacher. But I sort of fell into it. As I mentioned earlier, I was studying for a PhD in music psychology when I started teaching Swedish, and I had been studying musicology previously. I was all about music in those days, as well as a little bit of psychology.

When I started teaching, I felt really embarrassed that I was teaching Swedish with no qualification other than being a native speaker of the language. I felt like I was faking it. But I have always been interested in languages, I had high grades in Swedish and English from school, and I had also done a teaching degree for higher education (which was for teaching in general, not for teaching a language per se). However, I still felt I shouldn't bring up the fact that I was really doing a PhD in something unrelated.

After a few years, I did mention it to a few students and started talking about the links between music and psychology and learning a language. Being into music, I have always loved dialects because of their musical elements. I'm also deeply passionate about integration, and I see language as a powerful tool to integrate. This is me. I am a language teacher with a particular passion for the musical and the psychological sides of languages, along with integration and identity. This is my niche, my culture add. This is something that makes me stand out.

How to stand out as an online language teacher

You need a niche. Actually, you may even need a micro-niche.

You might be wondering what on earth a micro-niche is. Let's take a step back and look at the idea of *core markets*, *submarkets* and *niches*, and why it can be difficult to position your future language-teaching business in anything other than a smaller niche.

WHAT ARE CORE MARKETS AND SUBMARKETS?

Core markets are extensive areas like health, relationships, finance and education. As these markets are so broad and general, many *submarkets* have developed within each core market. In the health core market, submarkets may include weight loss or strength training; dating advice or parenting are potential relationships submarkets. For education, language education is a relevant submarket. I would be willing to argue that language education now functions as its own core market and each language (French, Spanish, English) is a submarket of that core market.

What submarket does your future business fit into right now? You might think that language education is enough. You're a French teacher, right? That's what you do. But building a sustainable online business in a submarket is difficult, as there will be too much competition there.

WHAT ARE NICHES AND MICRO-NICHES?

The next level down is a niche, which is a slightly narrower focus within a submarket. For a language teacher, a niche might be teaching English for academic purposes, business German, or teaching French to children.

Ask yourself: in which niche do I fit?

If you teach a language that is relatively 'small' (as for me, as a Swedish teacher), you might do well in a niche. But if you teach a more widely spoken language, chances are that this niche is quite crowded with competition. This is where micro-niches come in. This is an even narrower focus, where you can carve out a spot for yourself and become an expert.

Here are some examples of micro-niches in language teaching:

- Learn to watch films and TV shows in [insert language] without having to read the subtitles
- Learn [insert language] like a minimalist (I haven't tried this myself, but Eurolinguiste has a blog post about this approach – a link is available in the references at the end of the book)
- [insert language] for introverts and nervous speakers
- Accent reduction – speak like a [insert nationality]
- Conversational coaching for migrants coming to [country/countries]

- [insert language] online movie/book club
- Creative writing in [insert language]
- Job interview secrets in [insert language]
- [insert language] for busy executives
- [insert language] for parents

In the book *Blue Ocean Strategy*, Kim and Mauborgne talk about the fact that most markets and submarkets are 'red oceans'. The metaphor of a red ocean is a market or submarket full of blood from sharks feeding off the same pool of fish. These markets and submarkets (and sometimes also niches) already exist; there's a lot of competition within them.

A blue ocean, on the other hand, is an unknown area where demand is created. It's easy to see that submarkets and niches develop as a reaction to a red ocean in a market. It gets too crowded and too competitive, so people start inventing new and more specialized areas. The first teacher who taught Spanish online, for example, created a blue ocean with no other competitors. But as more and more people saw their success, they joined and that ocean slowly became redder.

What many people do when they start a business is they look around, see others doing well in their niches, and establish their business in the same area. But as you can now see, what these people are doing is stepping into someone else's blue-ish ocean and making it redder.

I would recommend that you instead look for micro-niches in your area and try and come up with a new one. A new blue ocean, just for you, where you can thrive. If you jump into an already red ocean, you'll be forever competing with others and you'll have a really tough time.

When you start looking around at other teachers in your submarket or niche (which you should definitely do), you'll be able to see what they teach, how they position themselves, how they market themselves and what they sell. This will give you tons of inspiration and will make it easier to see how you fit in. It will also stop you on the shore from jumping into waters that are too bloody.

IS IT BAD FOR BUSINESS TO NOT SERVE EVERYONE?

This idea of really narrowing down might seem limiting at first. Many language teachers feel that they want to help as many students as possible. Isn't it bad for business to offer something that not everyone wants? Well, actually, no. Apart from the fact that struggling in crowded waters is stressful and exhausting, there are two other important reasons why a narrower focus is a good idea.

Firstly, by having your own unique spot in your area, you can complement other teachers in your field. This means that your competitors can instead become your potential partners; you can collaborate with them. This in turn will make it much easier for you to present yourself to a wider audience (by guest blogging, joint webinars, joint live shows/podcasts, and so on) and attract more students.

I have a personal story about this. I met another Swedish teacher in my local area. We became friends and we really clicked. We started trying to figure out how we could collaborate, because we really wanted to do something together. But it was so difficult, as we were doing the exact same thing! Almost anything we came up with would mean that we would be competing against each other. We were in the same ocean. More recently, I met a Swedish singing teacher who I'm collaborating with to create pronunciation courses. Swedish is quite vowel-heavy, so coming at it from the perspective of singing is really interesting. I have also recently linked up with a person in the US who sells courses for people who want to find their Swedish ancestors and we're looking at ways to collaborate.

I would really recommend that you look around, see what other teachers are doing within your language, and see if you can find a way to create your own micro-niche: a blue ocean which would complement what they do. That way, you can later befriend them and create fun and exciting joint ventures that will be a win-win for you both. There's more about this in Chapter 10.

Secondly, having a micro-niche it will make it so much easier when you're creating your material, your marketing content and your brand. Everything will be much clearer in terms of design, core message and how to define what you offer. You'll be more visible and relevant, and you'll attract more students.

Think about how much there is to master for someone who wants to learn a language. The four main skills, lots and lots of different grammar points, specific pronunciation, culture, media, and so on. If you try and cover everything, your business will soon become diluted, scattered and also difficult to keep track of. It's much better to drill down and become an expert in a specific area. And also, you don't need all the students in the world to make your business successful!

HOW TO IDENTIFY A MICRO-NICHE

There's one important aspect to finding your micro-niche, and that is finding what your potential students really need and want. It's all very well to find a slim niche, but if no one wants what you have to offer, you won't have a viable business. You need to listen to what students want and what they're asking for, and then design services and products that solve their problems. If you can offer something that solves a problem that language students have, they'll come to you and do business with you.

The entrepreneur Russell Brunson uses a few questions to establish whether that field has space for a new business. You'll need to ask the questions to the submarket (or niche), as you'll be attracting people from that market into your new blue ocean. You don't have to literally ask other people these questions, just ask yourself and see what you think the answer would be.

If the language you're teaching is a bit smaller, you can imagine asking these questions to the people who are learning your language. If the language you're teaching has already split up into defined niches, and you have chosen yours (for example, business English), imagine asking the questions to that market.

Five questions to think about

1. If people in a submarket/niche are going to take a step over to your new business, they need to feel excited about it. Do you think people in this area would be excited about your new idea?

2. People also need to be really passionate. Find out if there are groups on social media, videos, blogs, podcasts and online forums available for this submarket/niche.

3. Do people seem willing and able to invest in information and 'how-to' advice? Being only willing but not able will not make students pay for your services, neither will being able but not willing, so you need people to be both.

4. Are there events available in this area? If there aren't, you might find it hard to get students to attend online training events, if that is a route you would like to go down. Find out if there are online seminars and conferences, for example.

5. Are there any celebrities and experts in this area? Even though you're going to carve out a unique spot within this ecosystem and complement the people who are already there, it will be much easier for you if there are established people out there who can sustain a business in this field. It's an indication that the market already exists.

Listening in

Another way to explore opportunities for micro-niches is to search out your submarket, listen in and really pay attention. Your goal is to identify what people's problems and difficulties are and see if you can design a solution. Because you're looking to establish yourself in a micro-niche, people online (or in the real world, for that matter) won't be talking about the service or product you'll be offering, because they won't know that it exists yet. But the problem that they have exists. It's your job to find out what they need. Here are some ways you can do this:

Join social media groups

- Make a list of social media groups in your submarket and join them. Then spend some considerable time sifting through questions and answers. This will reveal some of the big issues that people have and what they are looking for.

Read blog posts

- Search for blog posts about your topic and read any comments below to see what people say.

Watch YouTube videos

- Same process as with blog posts; pay close attention to what people say in the comments.

Find books in online bookshops

- Again, look at the reviews and comments and see if people express that they are missing something.

Look on other online forums

- Search for questions about your submarket on platforms such as Quora, LinkedIn and Reddit, for example.

This can be an intense research process, so make sure you note down all the questions people are asking. When you have done this, you'll find that you're getting a grasp of what the main problems are. This will give you new ideas on micro-niches you can develop. It might also be that someone else has created a micro-niche in another language, but perhaps this has not yet been done in your language.

Finding Your Why

After considering these aspects of identifying a micro-niche, it's time to talk about you. You may think that you should just simply choose the most profitable area, and that this will guarantee success. This is a mistake; the most profitable area may not be the one you're most passionate about. And remember this; unless you're passionate about something, you'll be overtaken by someone else who is.

You need to find your mission, your 'why'. Your mission is something that you passionately believe in, which you will use as an underlying thread in everything you do. Your mission should get you excited to get out of bed in the morning and be something that you can passionately talk about with students as well as your friends. When your mission becomes clear, it will be much easier to create content and material for your online business.

You may be familiar with Simon Sinek's TED talk 'Start with Why', or his book by the same name. If not, watch his TED talk immediately (it will only take five minutes).

In his TED talk, Sinek describes how conventional businesses often start with describing what they do, followed by how they do it. It's a conventional 'features and benefits approach'. For a language teacher, it might sound something like this:

> I am a French teacher. I offer affordable French lessons online, taught via Skype and by using bespoke learning material. Learn how to speak fluently with me. Book your first lesson today!

This is a typical 'what' description, followed by 'how'. Now let's look at how a description that starts with 'why', followed by 'how' and 'what', could sound:

> I believe in global communication across borders as a way to solve conflicts. By using online tools, I help politicians and executives and other professionals to negotiate and express themselves with clarity and integrity in French. I offer one-to-one sessions in advanced professional French online.

Which one of these do you think sounds more interesting, if you're an adult student looking to develop your professional French (even if you're not a politician or an executive)?

Stop here for a moment and ask yourself: what do I stand for? What are my beliefs?

Of course, wanting to learn a language does not necessarily have to involve someone's values and beliefs. But, when a potential student's values and beliefs align with the ones we express, they are much more likely to do business with us again and again. It becomes more than just a transaction of money and knowledge. It becomes an expression of an identity; what they believe in.

It's a bit like when you buy something eco-friendly, or organic. You're much more likely to stay loyal to a brand or a service provider if they share what you believe in, even if someone else offers you a better price. It makes us feel good when what we do is about something bigger than just ourselves.

Your why-statement should be refined into a sentence like this:

To _____, so that _____.

The first part will contain the contribution you make to others. The second part will contain the impact of your contribution.

Remember that this statement needs to be timeless and run through both your personal and professional life. Therefore, you can't create a why-statement like 'To teach students online, so that I can work from home.' Firstly, it isn't really an impact of your contribution to be able to work from home. It's more of a personal and practical circumstance, facilitated by teaching online. Secondly, you may not always work from home. This might change in the future. Therefore, you need to go deeper and create a why-statement that can guide you and live alongside you for the rest of your life.

It's not about creating an aspiration of what you want to become. Your why-statement is something that is essential and unique to you. It is something that has always been there and will always be there; it's your core. This why-statement will help to keep you on the right track as you move forward on your Language Teacher Rebel journey. People don't buy what we do, they buy why we do it.

Your Culture Add

Ask yourself this: who am I? (Don't panic and develop a full-blown existential crisis now, bear with me!)

What is your story? What are the things that have shaped you over the years? What are some other things that you love doing?

It took a long time before I was brave enough to start promoting myself as I actually am, but when I finally did, I was contacted by many students who said they had chosen me specifically *because of* my background. Maybe they too were interested in music. Or psychology. Or dialects. Or they liked my take on languages as something bigger than just verb tables and the grammar drills (although I love them too). Not all my students share these interests, but they're something that makes me unique, just because of who I am. And I can use that.

There's no one just like you and this is what you need to nurture as a Language Teacher Rebel. So ask yourself, what is your Culture Add? Consider the following elements, to try and formulate your Culture Add:

- Your cultural advantage
- Your circumstances
- Your identity
- Where you have been and why
- What you have achieved and how
- Who you have helped along the way
- Who and what you have taken a stand for.

The problem that most of us have is that we usually don't see our own unique abilities and what we are good at. We take them for granted. They feel so natural and instinctive to us that we feel that they surely cannot be something that other people would be willing to pay for.

But the thing is this: you have been blessed with ideas, gifts and talents, and through your background and your experience you have developed skills that you can use to serve others. Other people need your language-teaching skills. And they are just waiting for you to find your voice and become a Language Teacher Rebel, so you can start helping them.

You can explore your passions by trying Daniel Priestley's method of completing any of the following statements:

- _____ is what I believe people need right now.
- The relationship between ___ and ___ has always made me feel excited.
- Linking _____ and _____ is something I've always found intriguing.
- Now is a great time for _____.

The biggest hurdle you're most likely to face throughout this process is being comfortable with positioning yourself as an expert in what you do. You may feel like you don't have the right skills (in IT, marketing, teaching, creating learning material or marketing material, etc.). You may feel that you don't know enough. But you don't need to know everything in order to get started. As long as you know a little bit more than someone else, you can help them.

Having an entrepreneurial mindset means being comfortable with starting something and not knowing where it will end. It means being ok with learning as you go. This is also the best approach when you run a business, as it means you can stay lean and change direction if you need to. You won't get stuck in a rigid model that doesn't work. Technology changes, people's needs change, the world changes all the time. You need to surf along and ride the waves as they turn up. It's an ongoing process and you need to stay flexible. Therefore, you won't know what your business will look like in two years' time. And that is a good thing!

Your Pitch

Now you're ready to create bigger statements about what you can do for your students. Focus on filling in these blanks:

I believe in/My passion is…   [Why-theme]

I help…   [Student]

to…   [What they will learn]

so they can…   [Benefits]

For example, my why-statement looks like this:

> To inspire communication and cultural exchange,
>
> so that we can build bridges and increase empathy and understanding.

I have used a theme of communication, cultural exchange and building bridges to communicate what I believe in, to make a bigger statement that also includes what I do and the benefits of that. My bigger statement looks like this:

> I believe in communication, cultural exchange and building bridges.
>
> I help language teachers and wannabe language teachers to set up their own online language-teaching business, so they can share their language and culture across the world.

What is yours?

This will become the core element of your pitch. Your pitch is incredibly important. You might think of a pitch as something that innovators use when they want to secure large-scale investment (as in the TV programme *Dragons' Den/Shark Tank*), and you might think that it feels too commercial or corporate. But a persuasive pitch inspires people. It opens doors.

Consider this: most people you interact with have a network of over 250 people. A great pitch will make people remember you and recommend you to others. If you really inspire them, they may tell their friends about you, or even post on social media about you. Or they may offer to help in some way. You're actually pitching every time someone asks you what you do for a living! Next time someone asks you what you do, don't reply 'I'm a language teacher.' Instead, start the sentence with the pitch structure: 'My passion is… I help… to… so they can…

A great pitch will also guide you in your content and material design, when you write copy and blog posts, and ensure you're focused and clear in your communication with the world.

If you try out a pitch on someone and don't get the response you were looking for, don't worry. It might be that you have expressed yourself a bit unclearly. Perhaps what you meant to say didn't quite come out the way you wanted it to. It takes practice! Or it could be that what you said doesn't resonate with the other person. If so, that's fine too! You can't please everyone. Those who don't share your beliefs are not people that you'll be working with in the future anyway. Just move on and know that there is someone else out there with whom your message will resonate.

It's good to practise your pitch regularly, and meeting people you don't already know is a great opportunity to do so. When someone asks you what you do, try out your pitch. If you do this, you'll be well rehearsed and ready to go if and when you get a bigger opportunity to talk about your work.

When you can talk about your 'why' and effortlessly describe your bigger statements with clarity and confidence, opportunities will start to pop up. When they do, people who are interested will want to know more about you and how they can work with you.

Summary

- Identify your micro-niche by examining submarkets and niches.
- Listen in online to what people's difficulties and problems are.
- Create your why-statement.
- Explore your Culture Add.
- Craft a pitch.
- Take every opportunity to practise your pitch; you never know when an opportunity will come your way.

5

The Five-Step Language Teacher Rebel Roadmap

At this stage, perhaps you're thinking 'Great! I can teach online!' This is how I started too. But this is not just a book about teaching online. It's not only about using online tools to teach. Being a Language Teacher Rebel doesn't mean just working for another language school (and then happening to teach online). Being a Language Teacher Rebel means having your own business, being an entrepreneur and selling services and products directly to students.

By encouraging you to follow the Five-Step Language Teacher Rebel Roadmap, I am empowering you to set up your own business teaching online. I want you to create your own house, on a plot that you have staked out. In this chapter, I'll give you an overview of the Roadmap, and in the chapters that follow, I'll give you detailed advice on what you need to do at each step.

There are five steps that you will follow, in order to set yourself up as a Language Teacher Rebel. Here's an overview:

Step 1: The Quick Tech Set Up

1. Set up an email list and an email address.

2. Set up teaching tools (video conferencing, cloud computing).

3. Set up a Facebook/Instagram page (and maybe a community group).

4. Set up a payment system.

Step 2: The Quick Marketing Material Creation Blitz

1. Create information about yourself and take some pictures.

2. Create a Lead Magnet and content upgrades.

3. Create some Pillar Content.

4. Create a Content Planner.

Step 3: Early Growth – Evolving and Engaging

1. Create better content.

   i. Learn to use tools for creating video and visual content.

   ii. Create more texts and articles.

2. Engage with your online community.

3. Keep your email list warm but not 'spammy'.

4. Gather reviews.

Step 4: Developing and Investing

1. Set up an online booking system.

2. Set up a website.

3. Optimize your website.

Step 5: Flourishing with Momentum

1. Develop more content.

2. Get started with videos and live streams.

3. Build partnerships.

4. Create automations.

When you follow these steps in order, you will build a solid foundation for your online language-teaching business, while quickly getting your business up and running. You will position yourself as a competent expert within a specific field. You will create powerful content and attractive services and products, set up useful tools to work with, and find humanistic ways to connect with your audience. In the rest of this chapter, I'll give you an insight into and an overview of each step, before diving deeper into each of them in the following chapters.

Step 1: The Quick Tech Set Up

During this phase, you will be setting up the minimum tech tools so you can get started teaching online.

The first thing to do is to set up an email address and an email list. One of your central goals when you run an online business is to grow and nurture your email list. More on that later.

You will set up video conferencing (for example, Skype/ Zoom/Teams) so you can deliver your lessons live. You will also set up a cloud-based file system, like Dropbox or Google Drive, and organize it for your online business.

You will then create a Facebook/Instagram page and a community group, to start growing a community online. This will help you to find new students and build trust in you as a teacher.

Finally, you will set up a payment system, so you can accept payments online. You are officially up and running!

To get started straight away with this stage, go to Chapter 6.

Step 2: The Quick Marketing Material Creation Blitz

Your next step will be to quickly create some marketing material, so you can start to share valuable content online and draw people to your email list and your social media channel(s).

First of all, you will need to create some written information about yourself, what you offer and how you can help people. You also need some pictures of yourself.

Next you will be creating a Lead Magnet. A Lead Magnet is a free product that people can download in return for their email address. It's a way for you to show your expertise and how you can help, and a strategic way to grow your email list.

You will also need to create some written 'Pillar Content' and content upgrades to go with it. Pillar Content consists of valuable written articles that you can share with your email list, or post as blog posts or on social media. There are certain things that are worth creating early in the process, as prospective students will share a need for them. A content upgrade is a smaller free product that people can download in return for their email address.

During this phase, you will also create a couple of social media images, so you can use them as background photos on other social media channels.

Finally, you will also set up a Content Planner and start planning what content you will share with your audience and when.

At this stage, you will start getting interest from prospective students and start getting bookings (if you haven't already).

If you already have your basic tech set up and want to start creating marketing material, go straight to Chapter 7.

Step 3: Early Growth – Evolving and Engaging

Once you have some paying students, it will be time to evolve. You'll keep working on your marketing online, sharing content and drawing people onto your email list. You'll learn how to create better content to share with your followers. You'll also learn how to keep your community engaged.

You'll continue to nurture your email list. And you will gather any reviews from previous students and incorporate those into your marketing material.

If you've already completed Steps 1 and 2, go straight to Chapter 8 to find out how you can grow further.

Step 4: Developing and Investing

Alongside all the aspects that you have put in place in Steps 1–3, during this phase you will be able to invest in a few things that will help your business grow (as you'll now have some money coming in from your online teaching).

You may consider upgrading to a paid booking system, so you can access the useful features they offer, which in turn will offer your students a better service. You may consider setting up a website if you don't have one, or updating and optimizing the one you already have. All this is covered in Chapter 9.

Step 5: Flourishing with Momentum

At this stage, you'll have a growing online teaching business, and you'll continue to grow and develop. You'll develop more content and start refining your Product Ecosystem – where one product or service naturally leads to another.

If you haven't already, you'll start to explore creating videos and doing live streams on your social media channels. You'll also start to seek partnerships with others, collaborate and design more automations.

You can find out more about this in Chapter 10.

In the last chapter of the book, I'll go into a bit more detail about best online teaching practices, based on my experience. I'll show you how you can profile your students using the Six Characters of Drama, and through this knowledge decide what exercises and activities you use in your teaching.

Summary

The Language Teacher Rebel Roadmap includes the following five steps:

1. The Quick Tech Set Up

2. The Quick Marketing Material Creation Blitz

3. Early Growth – Evolving and Engaging

4. Developing and Investing

5. Flourishing with Momentum

6

The Quick Tech Set Up

As you start on your Language Teacher Rebel journey, there are a couple of things you should set up straight away. When you have these in place, you can start accepting paying students, and you will also have a basic foundation from which you can start marketing what you do.

Email address

Set up an email address that is separate from your personal one. You can easily set up a free email account, and just call it sarahenglishteacher@XXX, or something along these lines (or something more fun!).

You can also opt for the **two-step email sequence**. Many people will contact you and ask the same things: 'What's your schedule like?', 'What books do I need?', 'Can I get a receipt?' You can set up an automated reply, so you don't have to write the answers to these questions again and again. Remember, emailing is working for free, so you want to limit that. Here's how to do it.

AUTOMATED EMAIL 1

Set up one email address that is completely automated. Once you have set it up, activate the 'vacation setting'. Then, write a reply where you say:

> 'Hello and welcome; thank you for your email. I offer
> _____. They cost _____ and you can view my

schedule here:_____. Some common questions that
students often ask are _____. Here is how you book
lessons with me: _____, Here is how you pay: _____',

and so on.

Right at the bottom, add:

'If you have further questions, please contact me on my
teacher email _____, this is an automated reply'.

This will filter out probably 80 per cent of all the first-time
student questions, and you can focus on answering the more
specific ones that come through to your second email address.
Most students will not need to send you another email and
will go straight through to booking.

You could also consider adding a photo in this email, or even
a little introductory video for a more personal touch.

This is the first email address you give out; it's the one that
should be visible on your website/social media/business card,
etc. And you should (ideally) never check this email account.

If you want to see an example of this, send an email to
iwanttolearnswedish@gmail.com.

AUTOMATED EMAIL 2

Next, set up a second email address, which is the one that you
actually check. You should activate vacation settings for this
email address too. Here you could write something along the
lines of:

Thanks for your email.

Due to a heavy teaching workload, I am currently
checking and responding to emails once a day at 5 p.m.
Monday–Friday.

If it's really urgent and cannot wait until 5 p.m., please contact me on my mobile xxxx xxxxx.

Thank you for understanding this move to greater efficiency and effectiveness.

It helps me accomplish more to serve you better. :)

*Are you a new student interested in starting language lessons? Do you need information about the lessons, including payment details? *Please email me first on [your first automated email address].

This is useful, because your students will get an immediate response and they will know their email has been received. They will also be more patient with you for not replying straight away. This means you can check your emails less often, so you'll waste less time. I think I have only been contacted by phone once or twice during the last couple of years. Trust me, most people are very respectful.

The downside of having a two-step email sequence is that some people may contact your first email but then not follow through to your second email if they still have questions. Some might feel that it's too impersonal. I have used this system for many years and overall it has worked very well. But if you feel that you would like to give it a more personal touch, only set up automated email 2 (but keep the auto-reply on!).

Set up an email list

I have to admit, for a long time I ignored this. I didn't really understand what it was all about. I think at some point I did have a subscribe button on my website, and I think some people subscribed, but I had no idea what to do with it all.

I don't think I even knew where to find the email addresses that had subscribed! I have since started to realize how immensely important it is to build an email list.

What is an email list? It's a list of email addresses that people have given consent for you to contact them on. You should use an email program for this (not just your own list in a spreadsheet), such as Mailchimp or ConvertKit, for example.

Why is it important to have an email list when you have your own business? Here are two compelling reasons:

You don't own social media, so don't build your house on someone else's land.

If you have some followers on social media, great. But what if something changes on these platforms? They can change the algorithms and all of a sudden your followers might not see what you post. What if the platforms get hacked and go down (as Facebook and Instagram did in March 2019, for example)? If you don't want to be vulnerable, you must build your own email list.

It's also the easiest way to market. Writing emails is easier than designing social media posts. It's a great way to reach people who have already expressed an interest by opting in, and provide with useful things to show what you can do. Some of these people will become your future students.

One popular web-based program that you can use is Mailchimp. You can create email templates and landing pages. A landing page is a stand-alone website where people can subscribe or register for something by giving you their email address. You can use this type of program to offer a free download, for example, and set up certain workflows. A workflow in Mailchimp is when you tell the program to take a certain action depending on what a person is doing. If someone subscribes to your email list from your website, you might want an automatic welcome email to go out to them.

If you have set up a landing page where people can sign up to download a free cheat sheet, you want them to be added to your email list and for the cheat sheet to be made available to them. It can take a bit of time to get set up and to get used to the way the workflow works and what you can do, but the program is powerful and worth the time.

Another popular option is ConvertKit. At the time of writing this book, I'm using Mailchimp for my Swedish teaching and ConvertKit for Language Teacher Rebels (just because I like trying different things!). It works the same way as Mailchimp; you can set up landing pages, opt-in forms and create automations (which are the same as the workflows in Mailchimp). For more details on the current tools that I'm using, visit my website annelihaake.com.

When you start working with email list programs, you also need to be aware of GDPR. This is a European privacy law approved by the European Commission in 2016, and it applies to anyone in the EU region, or anyone collecting digital data from someone in the EU region. The GDPR regulates, among other things, how individuals and organizations may obtain, use, store, and eliminate personal data from someone in the EU region. If you don't live in an EU country, you need to be aware of and maintain an up-to-date knowledge of the data protection regulations in your country too.

One of the things you should make sure of is that people who opt in to your email list really want to be there. This is a good thing. You only want people there who are really interested in you and what you can offer. They need to explicitly opt in (not untick a box to opt out). A good method is to use a double opt-in when they sign up. This means that they opt in, then receive an email where they have to confirm, and only after they have done that will they be added to your email list. You can set this up in your email program. You can only use their email addresses for what they signed up for. For example, if they signed up to your newsletter to hear from you, you're not allowed to give their email address to anyone else. They must also be able to unsubscribe at any time. Email programs will have a link at the bottom of any email, where a subscriber can unsubscribe. And your wording should make clear what they're signing up for (i.e., your email list), so they know when they download something from you that they may receive future emails from you.

Set up teaching tools

- Video conferencing
- Cloud-based file hosting

Platforms such as Skype, Zoom and Microsoft Teams are examples of good video-conferencing tools for delivering live tuition. They are all commonly used, and many people already have their own accounts; if not, it's very easy to set one up. You can also chat, share screens and drag-and-drop documents and photos into the comment section that your student can open and save. Some of these platforms also have breakout rooms and recording options.

Dropbox, Google Drive and One Drive are file-hosting systems that offer cloud storage and file synchronization. I personally use Dropbox as backup (it automatically backs up all your documents), and also as an alternative place to get to my documents if I am not on my laptop. I also use it every day as a tool for sharing files with my students, by giving them a link to a Dropbox file that they can download (instead of doing the transfer in real time over Skype/Zoom or emailing). Check the terms and conditions for the exact details of free and paid offers, as well as the limitations of each platform.

Arrange a folder for each student, where you keep a lesson log where you record when you had a lesson, what you did during the lesson, and what homework you have given your student. You can also save any homework your student sends you into this folder.

Set up a social media channel

Before you start selling, you should serve. You should aim to help people and share your ideas and expertise with them. One of the best ways to do this is to set up a community somewhere on a social media platform. You can host an online community where people can join you. You can offer help and support and connect with them. An online community is also an excellent place to listen in and take stock of what people who are interested in your area of expertise really want and need.

BUT (and this is a big but) you should not attempt to set up an online community of your own if you have not been a part of a community on that platform before. Each platform works in a unique way; there are unwritten rules and etiquettes on each social media platform. If you have little social media experience, you can inadvertently come across in a negative way. So, if you have not been a part of an online community or an online group, your homework for now is to join one. Become an observer first, see how members behave and learn the 'lingo' and the etiquette of that platform. This way, you'll be more familiar and confident when you set up your own account.

FACEBOOK AND/OR INSTAGRAM

Two of the most popular social media channels are Facebook and Instagram. You are probably familiar with them both, but here's some basic information:

Facebook is a huge platform with over 2 billion users. You can create a business page and you can also start communities (groups) there. You can share text, images, videos and links. You can direct message with users and you can live stream video on your business page and into groups. Here you'll have 'followers' of your business page, and 'members' in your group.

Instagram is a large photo- and video-sharing social network (owned by Facebook) with around 1 billion monthly active users. You can make a business profile and share photos and videos as posts, stories or reels. You can communicate with others ('followers') through comments under posts and through direct messages. When you post, hashtags are an important feature in order for people who don't follow you to see your content.

At this stage, if you wish, you can:

- Set up a Facebook and/or Instagram page for your business.
- Set up a Facebook group, which will become your first online community.

The Facebook page is a bit like a shop window. Here you can post text, pictures, videos, share links, and so on. There are many things you can add to your Facebook page, but here is the minimum requirement for it to look active:

- Cover photo
- Profile photo
- Services you offer
- 'About' section (including 'Story')
- Newsletter (to plug in to your email list, so people can subscribe)
- Page button (could be 'Book now' if you have a booking system, or just 'Contact me')

Your Instagram profile is also a bit like a shop window, that you build up with photos and videos. Here are some things you need:

- Profile photo/logo
- Name
- Short blurb about you
- Photos and videos for posting

You have space in your profile section for one external link (to your website, for example), and you can also add action buttons with links (for example, 'book now' with a link to your booking system).

Your Facebook group will be your little club/tribe where people who want to learn your language can hang out, ask questions and interact with you. You don't necessarily need to spend a lot of time in your group, and there are ways you can automate things you post (you can schedule posts several months in advance).

The group will help people to get to know you as a teacher. You can serve people and show that you are trustworthy, and you can also ask questions so you can find out more about what people want.

Here are some things you need to get started with a Facebook group:

- Group cover photo
- An 'About' section with a description of the group
- Some general rules for your group (e.g. etiquette)

You may also want to consider adding some questions that people need to answer before they join your group. This is a good way to make sure people who want to join are doing so for the right reason (and are not just spammers), and it can also be a great way to find out more about what they want out of the group. This, in turn, can give you some insight into what to post and also what products and services you could develop in the future.

Take a look at other platforms too, such as Clubhouse, and see how you could build communities on there. It's useful to always be on the lookout for new trends and platforms.

Set up a payment tool

You need a payment tool to receive payments online from your students. One easy and common payment tool is PayPal. You can accept payments via PayPal if your student also has a PayPal account, but if you sign up for a PayPal Business account (this is the one I currently use) you can also accept credit card payments for a fee. It's very easy to integrate PayPal into most booking systems. Your students will be taken to a PayPal page where they can either log in to their own PayPal account or use their credit card to make the payment.

Stripe is another option, which is also easy to integrate into most booking systems. This tool allows you to take credit card payments (also for a fee), without students having to leave the booking system website.

Other common options are Square, Klarna, Authorize.net and Braintree, although some of these are more expensive to use. One thing to remember when you choose your payment tool is to include the cost of the payment tool (a transaction fee, for example) into your price. In other words, set the price of your service or products higher, so it covers the payment tool price.

You can also ask people to simply transfer money to your bank account, although you will need to manually check that the money has arrived. This is a headache as it takes a lot of time and energy. I did this when I first started, but my life became so much easier when I set up a payment system, so I highly recommend doing that.

Set up a booking system

You could start with manually organizing your bookings and arranging dates and times via email. Or you could sign up for a free account with an online booking system, like Calendly, SimplyBook.me, or Acuity (which is the one I currently use). Free accounts always have some limitations, but it could be a start if you want to save your pennies until you have more paying students. You can also use something like Google Calendar to schedule appointments to begin with.

Another thing to remember is that with a booking system, your students will always pay you when they book their lesson, so you won't have to manually check that they have paid (which means it's more financially secure for you).

Summary

ACTION PLAN

- Set up an email address.
- Set up an email program.
- Set up teaching tools.
- Set up a social media channel.
- Set up a payment tool.
- Set up a booking system (which could be a free account to start with).

7

The Quick Marketing Material Creation Blitz

When you are offering something online, you need to show who you are, what you do and what your thoughts are on your topic. This is how students will get to know you and trust you. You need to create and share something online to show your presence.

That something is *content*.

The most important thing about the content that you'll create as a Language Teacher Rebel is that it must be *valuable* for your students. If it's not valuable, you'll just waste your time creating it and your students' time having to read it (or try and ignore it).

The content you'll create will show students what you can do and who you are. It will also be a part of your Product Ecosystem and allow you to create products that you can later monetize. It will be a part of your intellectual property. But above all, it will allow you to engage with prospective students and build their trust.

Anything that you can create, publish and share online can be regarded as content. It can be blog posts, e-books, downloadable PDFs, videos, audio recordings and images.

In this chapter, we'll look at what you should start developing straight away, so you can start marketing yourself online. We will also look at how to best organize and plan the creation of your content, and we'll consider two techniques that you can use to find new students quickly.

What type of content should I have?

You'll continuously develop content as a Language Teacher Rebel, but what I want to present here is a *Language Teacher Rebel Content Starter Kit*. This kit will include some written content and visual content. Once you have this starter kit set up, you can begin designing a content strategy and share your content on social media channels and elsewhere, so you can attract your future students as quickly as possible. This suggested starter kit is an accumulation of my own experience and expert tips and is something I would have loved to have had when I started out more than 10 years ago!

Just to be clear, this content will be your own creation, so it's different from any teaching material you may use when you teach (already published textbooks, workbooks, slides, grammar references, etc.). You'll probably use those materials too, but your own content will be used in your marketing and will allow your students to connect with you.

Create a Lead Magnet

A Lead Magnet is something that you'll give away for free (what we also referred to as a First Free Offer in Chapter 3), but it is more than just an article. When I say more, I don't necessarily mean it has to be more words (although it might be), but it needs to be a resource that you want to become known for as a Language Teacher Rebel.

It could be an e-book, a free email course, or a pre-recorded webinar/video lesson. The content should solve a specific problem for your student and should be so good that they can't stop talking about it. Here are some tips on how to create an e-book and a free email course.

E-BOOK

An e-book should be at least ten pages long. You can use this layout:

- A title page
- Introduction and overview
- Main content
    - Describe problem or language point.
    - Describe cause of problem.
    - Describe effects of problem.
    - Describe solution.
- Summary
- Where to find out more (contact details).

Or use a different structure if it fits your topic better. You can write it in Word or PowerPoint (or design it in Canva), for example, and then save it as a PDF. Don't forget to put your logo and website address on it! You can also place the copyright symbol (©) on any original piece of work you have created. The standard format would be to include alongside the copyright symbol the year of first publication and the name of the copyright holder, however there are no particular legal requirements to do it this way.

✸ EMAIL COURSE

An email course is a drip-fed sequence of emails (you can set this up to automatically send in your email program) that is designed to educate your prospective students and for them to get to know you better. Here are five simple steps for creating a free email course:

Step 1: Come up with the outline

- Your email course topic
- The course title
- A hashtag for it
- What people will learn by the end of your free email course

Step 2: Clarify your goal

Next, think about what your ultimate goal is for your free email course. Is it:

- To prep people to buy your future product/service?
- To sell your paid product/service?
- To learn more about your audience (when they answer your engagement/reply emails, you'll get ideas for your future products and/or copy writing)?

Step 3: Repurpose if you can

Think about how you can use some of the content you already have. Have you already got written content that can be used, perhaps from previous lessons? You don't need to start from scratch when you're creating your free email course!

Step 4: Create the emails

Your email course will have the format of informative blog posts. You can start by writing the emails as separate documents. Add videos or audio recordings to your course if you want. Your prospective students could receive one email a day for about a week. Here is an example of a seven-day free email course:

Email 1: Welcome and introduction

Welcome your subscriber, briefly introduce yourself and tell them what they can expect over the next few days, and advise them if they need to prepare anything. If you have a free community group or a free download, you can link to that here too.

Emails 2–6: Lessons

These five emails will teach them one thing each day about your topic.

Email 7: Conclusion

Round up the course and encourage your subscriber to take further action (for example, book a lesson with you/sign up to your online course). You can offer a discount if you want.

If you would like a workbook to take you through the process of creating a free email course, I have included one in my *Language Teacher Rebel Toolkit*. Go to library.teachyourself. com for more information.

Step 5: Set it up in your email program

The last step is to set up your free email course in your email program, such as Mailchimp or ConvertKit. You need to create 1) a landing page for your course, and 2) the content as a series of automated emails.

Connect the course to your landing page and set it up to drip feed one email every day after students have signed up. This means that when they sign up, they will automatically get your Welcome email, and 24 hours later they will receive email number 2, and so on.

PRE-RECORDED WEBINAR/VIDEO LESSON

Another option for a Lead Magnet is a pre-recorded webinar. Think of it like a pre-recorded lesson where the video shows slides and you talk over the slides (and maybe appear in a video 'bubble' in one corner of the screen, so students can see you when you talk).

You don't have to have slides in your webinar, you could just have yourself as a 'talking head', although it can be nice for people to read main points on slides, see illustrations, and follow along with what you are saying.

This is a much better option than giving away a trial live lesson for free. Why? Because you only have to design the lesson once, and then it does the work for you. It doesn't eat into your time that you could spend teaching or developing more material.

I have found Loom, Zoom and ScreenFlow for example, to be good options for recording this type of product, as you can record your screen (where you have your slides) and yourself as a video icon while talking in front of your screen. You may need to tweak a few things in a video editor afterwards.

Then create a landing page in your email program that gives people the link to your video. You can just link it to where it has been saved online, or where you keep the video in your file-hosting system (just make sure they can't download the file, unless you want them to). You can also upload it as an unlisted video on YouTube (so people can't find it without the link).

CONNECT YOUR LEAD MAGNET TO YOUR EMAIL LIST

The last (but maybe the most important) step is to set up your Lead Magnet so that people can give you their email address in order to download it. You can do this in your email list program (Mailchimp or ConvertKit, for example).

If you do this in the free version of Mailchimp, you may need two landing pages:

- One landing page where people can subscribe
- A second landing page where they can access your content upgrade

Instruct the first landing page to lead the visitor to the second landing page once they click on the subscribe button.

If you do this in ConvertKit, you can just upload the downloadable file to the first landing page, so they can download it straight away once they have subscribed.

The link to the first landing page is the one you will include in your posts to social media or your blog posts.

Create Pillar Content and content upgrades

Now you are going to create some *Pillar Content*. What I mean by Pillar Content is that the content you create will be the backbone of your business. This will be made up of four essential pillar articles and also four language-specific articles. Later you will create content upgrades for your language-specific articles (more about content upgrades below).

Writing Pillar Content articles will help you clarify your ideas and will also provide copy that you can use elsewhere (on your website, as a basis for a video or podcast episode, as a free download, as snippets for social media posts and more). And you only have to write them once!

FOUR ESSENTIAL GENERAL ARTICLES

Firstly, let's look at four essential general articles that you will be writing:

1. FAQ

2. Your Story

3. Common Pitfalls (and how to avoid them)

4. The Myth Buster

FAQ

This is a very helpful article of frequently asked questions that you can use and repurpose in many different formats in your business, and it's also great to refer to, or just copy and paste into emails for students. The text will be in the form of questions as the sub-headings, and then you write the answers underneath the headings. You can also include relevant links if you need to.

The FAQ for your specific business will depend on what products or services you offer, but here are common questions when teaching adults one-to-one online:

- How much does a lesson cost?
- What are your terms and conditions?
- Can I get an invoice or a receipt?
- What is your teaching schedule?
- How long will it take before I can speak decent Swedish?
- How do I know what my current level of Swedish is?
- What is your teaching experience and background?
- What can I expect from a lesson?
- What kind of material do you use? Do I need to get books?
- Do I need to do homework?
- Can I do anything to prepare for my lesson?
- Can I share a lesson with a partner/friend?

Before I created this content myself, I would sit and write individual emails to respond to people's questions as they came in. This took so long to do and took up time I could have been spending more productively.

Have a think about which of these questions relate to your products/services, and amend the list to suit your business. You can always add new questions and answers to your list as they come up.

Your Story

In this article, you'll tell your story. Talk about who you are, how you became a teacher who is passionate about what you are teaching, what you've been through to get there, why you think your topic is important, and so on. The text should tell the reader about your journey to where you are right now. But, it should not read like a fleshed-out CV!

Your story should be intimate and personal. It should include some tough times and challenges, or unusual details, so people can really get to know you and feel that you are a real human being. You can tell the reader about what you are passionate about, what you do outside of your teaching, and what you believe in. Try and aim for at least 500 words (but don't worry if it turns out much longer; that's fine!), which will take about two minutes to read. A nice way to frame it is to start the title with: 'How I...'.

Some people may find the idea of writing this type of article a bit self-indulgent. I can totally understand that! You may feel that your business is not about you, but about your students, your topic and your content. However, these types of articles are one of the most powerful stories you can create, because they resonate with people.

People want to know about you, the person behind a website or business. This information builds a high level of trust, which is important when someone decides to spend their money. They can see that there is a real, authentic person there that they can have a relationship with, not just stylish content.

Common pitfalls (and how to avoid them)

This article is about issues you have seen people struggling with and how to overcome those challenges from your perspective as a teacher. The exact struggles and challenges will depend on your micro-niche, but you can probably already think of some things that most of your students find hard.

The pitfalls could be something specific, like a grammar or pronunciation point. Or they could be something more general relating to the study process, like not setting aside enough time to revise, relying on Google translate, or underestimating how long it will take them to make progress.

If you come up with a lot of potential student challenges, you could split them into several articles (perhaps according to themes, for example, 'Common pitfalls when studying and how to avoid them', and 'Common pitfalls when learning new words and how to avoid them.'). You can keep these ideas in a document and write them up later. You don't need to write all of them at this stage, just pick one that you think your prospective students will find especially useful. Again, aim for a minimum of 500 words.

The Myth Buster

This is an article that 'busts' the top three to five myths that people believe about your topic. It could be a general article dealing with myths about learning your language, or even learning any language (for example, 'Adults struggle to learn a language', 'There is one optimal way to learn a language', 'Total immersion/living in a country is the only way to learn'). Or it could be something more closely linked to your micro-niche. Whatever the myths are, your goal with this article is to explain the myth and why it's not true. By challenging these misconceptions, you'll actually deal with the main fears and misconceptions that people have about your topic and help them overcome their doubts about why they should do business with you.

You can either structure the text by outlining the myth as a statement ('There is one optimal way to learn a language') and then write underneath why it's not true, or you can pose the myth as a question ('Is there one optimal way to learn a language?') and then address the myth under the question. If you have been doing your research into your micro-niche (as we talked about in Chapter 4), you'll know exactly what the most common myths about your topic are.

FOUR ESSENTIAL LANGUAGE-SPECIFIC ARTICLES

You are also going to create some essential language-specific articles, that relate more closely to your micro-niche.

Start by choosing three to four language-specific themes that relate to the topic that you want to teach. These can be very specific to your particular niche, but if you struggle to think of any, use these more generic ones to start with:

1. Culture

2. Grammar

3. Pronunciation

4. Vocabulary

Write one article for each topic (around 500–1,000 words each). If you want to write culture articles, you could describe traditional/seasonal events in places where your language is spoken and explain the history of these events and their related customs, including the specific vocabulary used. You could address, explain and provide tips on specific problems of grammar and pronunciation. Vocabulary articles could provide glossaries on specific themes or situations.

Create content upgrades for your language-specific articles

Next you are going to create a *content upgrade* for each article. If you are not already familiar with the concept of a content upgrade, this is a free download that you attach/link to from a blog post. Content upgrades should be super-useful and help people to save time, organize themselves, or get more detailed information about the topic. Even if you are not starting a blog right now (or ever), it's very useful to create these alongside your language-specific articles and you can use them in many other ways later on.

Here are some examples of content upgrades perfect for Language Teacher Rebels:

- Cheat sheets
- Glossaries, verb tables, scripts, etc.
- Checklists
- Printable worksheets
- Roadmaps/flowcharts/diagrams
- Vocabulary trackers
- Links to exercises (for example, links to a password-protected Quizlet set that you have created)
- Audio download
- Video download demonstrating a particular pronunciation.

Get into the habit of creating an accompanying content upgrade when you write a blog post or a text. Honestly, I wish I had thought of this when I started. It is of course possible to go back to older blog posts, update them and add a content upgrade to that post. But it's much easier if you create them both at the same time, as it saves you having to shoehorn a content upgrade in and trying to make it fit the blog post.

Finally, create a folder for all your articles, then save each essential language article together with its content upgrade in a separate folder, for example like this:

- Main folder
  - Essential language articles
    - Swedish possessive reflexive pronouns
      - Article: Best way to understand Swedish possessive reflexive pronouns
      - Content upgrade: Cheat sheet – possessive reflexive pronoun table
    - Swedish Midsummer
      - Article: How to celebrate Swedish Midsummer the Swedish way
      - Content upgrade: Glossary for traditional midsummer food and drinks

CONNECT CONTENT UPGRADES TO YOUR EMAIL LIST

Again, just as you did with your Lead Magnet, create landing pages for each content upgrade, so that you can capture people's email addresses when they download your material. Don't forget this step!

Create content about yourself

You need to create some content about yourself as well, so that you can use it online to show people who you are. But before we start with creating any new content in this category, we need to review any content that is already 'out there', and also remove or edit anything that you don't feel comfortable with. Are you aware of what comes up when you search for your name online? If not, it's time to search yourself.

ONLINE PRESENCE AUDIT

Firstly, search for your name on the internet and see what comes up. Are you on the first page, or even better, among the top three or four results? Have a look at any links or images that come up. Where do they come from? What comes up first? If you don't have a website yet, any images or articles are likely to come from other platforms, perhaps LinkedIn or Facebook. Have a look at them and see if they give the impression you want to create. Would they look good to a potential student? If not, you should probably remove them.

Secondly, go into Facebook specifically. Review your privacy settings on your personal profile and see what can be viewed publicly. This includes any comments that you have made under a post in a public group or on a public page. Delete any images or comments that you don't want your students to see (or if possible, change the privacy settings to private/friends only). Also, if you haven't already, set up a separate business page.

Thirdly, go into your LinkedIn profile and update any job titles and experience, and make sure your profile picture is up to date. Some people have a profile on LinkedIn that they rarely revise, so make sure yours is updated and that the job description matches what you want to do and is in line with your story.

Next, visit your personal Instagram profile, if you have one. If your personal profile is public, check to see whether the images you're sharing fit in with the story you're trying to tell. If they don't, consider changing your settings to private and set up a separate account where you share what you want your students to see (or one specifically for your business). Then repeat for any other platforms you may be registered on.

Now that you are satisfied with any content that might already be online, it's time to create some new visual content for your online teaching business.

PHOTOS

Start by taking a couple of headshots of yourself. Think approachable: not overly formal, and a white background is not required, but it should not be too casual either.

Next up, you will take some behind-the-scenes photos. People love behind-the-scenes photos. It brings that sense of you being a real person to the forefront, and people love getting a sneaky peak behind the curtains of a business.

Take ten behind-the-scenes photos. You can stage these photos to start with, so you have something to begin with. Later on, you can take more photos to add to this category. Here are some examples of pictures you can take:

- Pictures of your desk: from different angles, close ups, etc.

- Personal photos: a cup of coffee from your 'break'; yourself sitting in the sun outside between lessons; your favourite book; your favourite place in a country where your language is spoken.

- Pictures of you working: creating your essential language articles, for example, or other work in progress. These can be with you in the picture or a photo of the work itself (preferably both). Stage a few pictures of you teaching too.

- A handful of nice, more casual selfies

VIDEOS

Record a couple of short videos. If you have a smartphone you can use this to record. Most smartphones have great cameras these days, and the video doesn't have to be perfect. Just make sure the background is fairly plain to ensure the focus is on you and that you are looking decent.

- Introducing yourself and what you do (max. three minutes)
- FAQ videos (one per question); just do exactly the same as you did in your essential text (questions + answers)

If you want to add some fun videos into your starter kit too, why not record a couple of videos of yourself saying tongue twisters into the camera? I have posted some of these on social media in the past. They were super-short (15 seconds or so) and I ended up laughing as I failed to say them really fast, but people loved them and requested more.

How to organize and plan content creation

At this point, you might be wondering how on earth you'll have the time to create this amount of content. I can understand that it might feel a little overwhelming.

But it's worth spending this time in the beginning creating your content. Everything you create will save you time further down the line. You can use the content in many different forms, repackage it for different platforms, and you'll also have many templates that you can use if you want to create something new. What's more, you'll have a strong and powerful collection of materials that really establishes you as an expert Language Teacher Rebel in your field.

Once you have created this content, start drip-feeding it out via social media to drive traffic to you and your email list. Don't forget to post regularly in your community group too (if you have one)!

This last section of the chapter will present two ways to plan your content creation, sprinting and batching, and introduce the idea of keeping a content calendar.

SPRINT PLANNING

Most of us know what it feels like to have bigger projects in front of us. You look at them and do a bit here and there. You start something else and then try to come back to the bigger ones and really concentrate. And then you look back at your to-do list a month later, and the projects are still there, and it feels like you haven't made any progress. Let me introduce you to the idea of **sprints**, as a way to prioritize, start and finish things you need to get done.

The concept of sprints comes from the 'Scrum' framework devised by Jeff Sutherland, a framework initially popular when designing software, which has now become popular in other teamwork contexts. Even though the whole framework is designed for teamwork progress, the concept of sprints can be used by a single person to plan tasks and complete projects.

The idea of a sprint is to break bigger projects down into smaller chunks that you can complete in two weeks. During a sprint, you'll only work on this particular part of your project, which will allow you to make real progress. If you have a bigger project, you need to break it down into two-week sprints and complete these one by one.

How you define a sprint will depend on how much time you can spend on your task. So, for example, if you are completely free and don't have any other work to do, a sprint would be 80 hours (40 hours per week x 2 weeks). But if you can only spend, let's say, four hours per week working on your task, then one sprint would be eight hours. So you need to break down your projects into what are manageable sprints for you.

During a sprint, it's really important that you only work on completing that particular sprint. You are not working on trying to make a bit of progress on three different projects, instead you are starting and finishing one project. This is how people actually get things done.

Depending on how much time you can dedicate to a sprint, you may be able to write essential articles 1–5 in one sprint. Or another good sprint could be to get your photos and videos done. Or create your First Free Offer and a landing page in your email program. When you work in this way, you are really committing to getting it done, instead of doing a couple of photos a couple of times per week.

The process of sprint planning will also allow you to realistically plan out how long things are going to take. When you do your sprint planning, don't try and squeeze in one task in three days. Each sprint should be two weeks long. Make sure that the sprints are laid out in a logical order, too. So, for example, if you need to research online forums and groups to find out what people are asking for in relation to your topic, you need to do this before you can write your essential language-specific articles. Spend one sprint on trawling through forums and groups and collect data on what seem to be the biggest issues in your topic. After that, you can create a sprint where you write language-specific articles.

Aim to plan sprints for a three-month period, so six sprints in total. A three-month period is long enough for an overview of what you need to do to actually achieve something. Planning for longer than that rarely works. Things change along the way, and it's good to stay agile and be able to respond to feedback and new ideas.

BATCHING

Another good method of organizing what you want to do is to work on similar things at the same time. This is called 'batching'. Let's say that you are planning to take some photos or record some videos. Do them at the same time, as they require the same tools and the same kind of process. You may need to tidy up your office, find some nice props, and maybe rig a tripod for some photos and videos. It's better to do the prepping and rigging once, rather than having to set it up several times. This will save time. This also works well when you have several tasks that require the same program. Have a content design session, for example, where you create a lot of photos or documents in one go.

Batching allows your brain to focus on one type of task at a time, making you more productive. When your brain has to 'switch gears' all the time, you are slower and more prone to distractions. You might think that it's good to be able to multitask, but when you are multitasking, you are forcing your brain to 'task switch', which makes us tired and unproductive.

You can use the batching technique for your typical daily tasks (all the tasks in your life actually, not just work-related ones), and batch them to specific days. Of course, when you are sprinting on something, keep your focus on that.

⊗ CONTENT CALENDAR

The last thing that you should do is to set up a content calendar. This can be as simple as a spreadsheet where you plan and oversee what to post where and when. It's really useful to get used to working off a content calendar at this stage; it will be hugely helpful later on when you grow and expand.

In my *Language Teacher Rebel Toolkit*, I have included the exact content calendar that I use for my business.

Ways to find new students quickly

As you set up your business and start to gain followers, students will start to find you. But there are two ways you can super-charge this process and reach a bigger audience fast: guest posting and running webinars.

GUEST POSTING

Think about who might serve the same audience, but with a different service or product (in other words, not a competitor). You can approach this person/organization/ company and suggest a collaboration, for example guest posting on their blog.

You obviously need to write a high-quality article for this, but it's a great way to get you in front of new people. You can repurpose something you have already written as a part of your Pillar Content. You should also include some kind of free download as a bonus, and hook this up to your email program, so you can grow your email list.

You can also appear as a guest in other ways, for example as a guest on someone's podcast, or being interviewed by someone live on their social media channel. Again, include an offer of a free bonus that people can download.

WEBINARS

Another way to find new students quickly is to run a free webinar on a specific topic that you know many people struggle with. Focus on one thing that you can help them with, so they can walk away from their webinar with a quick win. You can market your webinar on social media (you can share it with everyone you know and ask them to share it too, or if you want you could spend a little money, perhaps £10–20 ($15–30) to start with, on a Facebook/Instagram ad).

Webinars can be very powerful, as you can show off your teaching and build trust, and your prospective students will feel like they are connecting with you.

You can either do a pitch-free webinar and just offer your audience something useful, or you can pitch your services at the end.

Make sure you get people's email addresses when they register (for example, via a landing page where they can get access to the webinar link once they have registered). You can run this kind of webinar on Zoom, for example, or as an unlisted live stream on YouTube.

Another useful thing is to record the webinar, so you can share it later if you want to. Or take small clips from it and use them in your marketing. If some of the participants are shown on the video, you'll need their permission before using any of the material in marketing. I have included a 'release form' in my *Language Teacher Rebel Toolkit* that you can use to get their consent. Otherwise, just make sure that you are the only person shown in the clips.

HOW TO FRAME THINGS YOU SHOW PROSPECTIVE STUDENTS

When you start to market yourself to audiences, you should take some time to think about who your ideal student is. Consider a specific person who would be interested in your micro-niche and would feel attracted to your 'why' statement. Where do they hang out online and offline? How do they talk (not in terms of the language they're learning, but in their mother tongue – how do they express themselves)? And most importantly, what real result can you give to that person if they study with you?

You can actually imagine this person as a real human being in front of you. Imagine one real person with one real problem that you could help to solve. As we've already talked about in the section on micro-niches, it's good to be targeted and specific. You shouldn't be trying to help everyone.

Then ask yourself the following questions about this imaginary person:

- What fears do they have? (What keeps them up at night?)

- What are three negative emotions they are experiencing and how could you help them with those?

- How are you different from other people in your field? (Draw on your culture add, your 'why' statement and your micro-niche.)

When you create material to share (whether it's blog posts, a webinar, social media posts, and so on), you need to imagine yourself speaking directly to this person.

WHERE TO FIND YOUR IDEAL STUDENTS

The easiest way is to start hanging out on one or two social media channels/online communities. Find a group in your niche and see if you can find your ideal student there.

Your job in these groups is to provide value in the comments. Explain, share useful tips, ask questions. Do NOT post any promotions or try and sell anything at this stage. You need to serve before you start to sell. If you immediately start posting about what you offer you will come across as 'spammy', and the admin of the group may even block you.

When you post questions or comments keep the language clear, simple, friendly and helpful. Use the same kind of language as others are using. If you make connections or if people ask you follow-up questions, you could offer to send them a private message. Again, no promotions at this stage, but you could send them a link to a really useful blog post on your website or somewhere where they can also see what you do. Or share something they will find helpful. Just point them in that direction, but without selling. You're just being helpful and kind.

Summary

ACTION PLAN

- Create a Lead Magnet.
- Create Pillar Content.
- Create content upgrades.
- Create content about yourself.
- Plan your content creation by sprinting and batching, and using a content calendar.
- Be clear about who your ideal student is and start hanging out where they hang out. Provide value and be helpful. No promotion.

8

Early Growth – Evolving and Engaging

Now that you have a few social media channels and some basic marketing material set up, it's time to start talking about what you can do to grow your business. During this early phase, it's important to maintain the systems and processes you have already put in place and keep engaging with your followers.

Creating better content – and more of it

When you're regularly creating content, you'll need some design-specific tools. Here are some tools that I have found very useful.

TOOLS FOR PHOTOS AND VISUAL POSTS

When I create anything on social media, I use Canva, but there are other programs available. Canva is an online graphic design tool with many options for social media posts. There is a free option that you can start with. One potentially annoying thing about social media posts is that they all have different dimensions. For example, Instagram posts are currently 1080px by 1080px for square posts and 1080px by 1350px for portraits. Facebook news posts' recommended size is 1200px by 630px, cover photos are 851px by 315px, and profile pictures 180px by 180px. If this is beginning to give you a headache (it did for me), you can upgrade your Canva account to Canva for Work, which allows you to resize any design you want and use custom dimensions. I usually use free versions of most programs and apps, but this was so worth it for me. You can upload your own pictures or symbols, create your own fonts, and they also have many templates that you can use for free or buy.

Speaking of pictures, you can find a lot of free stock photos on places like Pixabay, Adobe Stock Free Collection, or Pikwizard. Just be careful to not overuse stock photos, as they can sometimes look cheap and impersonal. Collect 30+ stock photos that you can use as backgrounds for social media posts. Make sure you check the terms and conditions, in case you need to include attributions in your post. If you are good at taking photos, you can of course use your own. Do not just pick a photo from an internet search! If you publish it without the photographer's explicit consent you can end up in trouble.

Try and collect photos (and put them into a specific folder on your computer) from these three categories:

1. Nature or cityscapes relevant to the language you're teaching

2. Typical foods or animals from the country/countries where the language is spoken

3. Background photos. These could be of some kind of material, like wood, stone, sand, water, or blurry pictures – these are great for creating social media posts with writing on top. When you look at materials and colours, try to select ones that feel relevant for the language you're teaching. For me, teaching Swedish, I have a lot of wood, Northern Lights, water and snow in my stock photo library.

Should you want to have a professional logo designed at some point, have a look at marketplaces like Fiverr, Upwork or Freelancer. (Fiverr is specifically for designers.)

TOOLS FOR VIDEOS

There is a wealth of video-making tools available. Here are some of the video tools that I, personally, have found useful.

If you record videos, you can just start with your mobile phone. You may want to buy a small tripod so you can put the phone somewhere and sit in front of it. If you have any video-editing software on your laptop, then start by using that (iMovie on MacBooks, for example). If not, you could try Animoto, which is a web-based video-editing tool. They have a free version, although their logo will be included at the end of each video.

Another fun video tool is Lumen5. In Lumen5, you can create videos from text. If you have a blog post that you would like to turn into a video, you can insert the text or a link to your published blog post. Lumen5 will then create a draft video, based on the text, which you can then edit and tweak as you want. You can upload your own photos or video clips, and you can also use some from Lumen5's own library. Lumen5 will automatically try and get pictures that match the text, but sometimes it doesn't work at all, so you might need to change a few things. But it's much easier than starting from scratch.

You can also add background music from their music library or upload your own (as long as it's not copyright-protected). The free version is slightly lower resolution and you do get their logo included right at the end, but I don't feel it's intrusive. You can then download the video from their website and upload it to Facebook or YouTube. I have created a few FAQ-based videos with Lumen5, like 'How long does it take to learn Swedish?', 'What should I do to prepare for my first Swedish lesson?', and so on.

GO DEEPER WITH YOUR ARTICLES

In Chapter 7, I talked about some of the essential articles that you should create. Now is the time to expand on these articles, so here are some ideas for other articles you could consider writing, as they work well as blog posts/articles for driving traffic to your site.

THE ULTIMATE GUIDE

This is an article where you outline, in seven to ten steps, a comprehensive guide to something that is relevant to your micro-niche audience. The guide topic will depend entirely on what your micro-niche is, and it should go into detail about something that your prospective students really need to know.

If you are teaching business English, for example, you could write an ultimate guide to how to prepare for a job interview and what to expect during an interview. It could include tips, tricks, steps, vocabulary glossary/useful phrases, etiquette tips, and so on. Or if your prospective students are people who are looking to relocate, it could be the ultimate guide to how to move to a country where the language is spoken, outlining the steps they need to take to apply for relevant visas, how to find a place to live, and including links to relevant authorities, companies, forums, and so on.

You could also make it more language-specific, for example the ultimate guide to learning your language, where you flesh out the steps that a student needs to take, what resources they will need, tips on how to manage their time when learning, and so on. Or keep it closer to your micro-niche, whatever that is.

If the topic gets really huge, you could break it up into a series of articles, but as with the articles above, try and keep them to 1,000 words minimum, ideally around 3–5,000.

TOOLS AND RESOURCES

This is an article that you create as a list with accompanying explanations of the tools or resources that are necessary for what you teach. If you are using specific teaching books, this could be a list of the most relevant language resources students will need. Explain in detail what each book does, how it's designed, what level it's for, and so on.

This article could also be a list of online resources that are useful for your students: apps, programs or other tech tools, for example. You could focus on language-specific tools (good flashcard apps, online dictionaries, etc.), but you could also include other tech tools that are useful for your students when they are studying (Zoom, Skype, Dropbox/Google docs for sharing, etc.). Or you could discuss other digital tools that they could use for immersing in the language (online radio channels, video or news channels, vlogs, etc.).

The goal of the article is to give an overview of the basic tools or resources that someone would need in order to learn what you teach.

HOW-TO TUTORIALS

These are step-by-step guides on how to use the kinds of tech that your students need in order to study with you. If you are going to run live teaching via Skype or Zoom, for example, write a tutorial on how to use that program. Or, if you sell an online course, you could write a how-to tutorial for any programs or apps you recommend students use. It could also be a tutorial on how to use a particular tool or resource from your Tools and Resources list. You can create tutorials in step/list form and include screenshots of relevant stages in the process.

A note on time: these types of articles can age quite quickly if the tech that you are using introduces an update. It's the only type of article in this list that can run the risk of not being evergreen. It's therefore worth keeping an eye on the technology and make sure to update the text/links/ screenshots when they need it (maybe once every six months). However, tutorials are much appreciated by students and provide a lot of value, so I think it's still worth doing.

THE CASE STUDY

While your case study could focus on one of your students, if you have learned a language yourself, you can be the subject. The article should explain how you or your student achieved a specific result within a specific time frame. Some details can be shared with your 'my story' article, but in a much more compressed and time-specific form. You could also present your case study in the form of an interview with the subject. The article could explain, for example, how your student learned the language you teach over a period of months or years, or how they learned to conjugate 20 verbs in an hour, or another achievement that relates to your language (and ideally your micro-niche).

If you're just starting out, it might not be possible to write a case study straight away. You may have to wait for some results to come in before you can write about them. That's totally fine. But make sure to keep this type of article in mind when you start teaching. Make notes of dates, methods, actions and achievements along the way, so you can write them up as an article later when you have more results. Perhaps you can capture a video/audio recording of your students at the beginning of their studies and again later on when they have achieved a goal (if you have their consent, of course).

You can also ask your students to take a selfie when they've achieved a goal (just after passing an official exam that you have been helping them to prepare for, or after a job interview, or when visiting a country where the language is spoken), and request permission to use it. Keep these ideas in mind throughout your teaching process, as you can create really powerful content that validates your business. It's even better if your student would be happy to be interviewed by you (either as audio only or on video).

Make sure you get your student's explicit written consent to publish the case study on your website and on social media, or anonymize the text so no personal details can be traced to your student. If you're recording it, ask your student to confirm the edited version in writing before you put anything out online.

TAKE A STAND

In this article, you have the opportunity to share something that you deeply believe in. It might be an opinion that is not shared by everyone else in your educational community, or it could even be something that you disagree with. It might be an issue you have with the way things are done in your field.

It could be the way something is traditionally taught, or the way it's assessed or marked, or it could be about a new trend in your area. It could be something more general to do with learning any language, or something much more specific. You'll take a stand and share your unique take on this aspect of your field.

It's absolutely fine if it's a bit controversial, but you don't have to try and come up with something contentious just for the sake of it. You can simply outline what your values and perspectives are on this particular topic. But if you have something that you believe in that you know not everyone agrees with, don't be afraid to share it. It's completely fine if some people disagree with you.

Taking a stand on something will position you as a thought leader in your area and will help establish your brand, your voice and your personality. It will also help you to attract the right students.

Inspiring your community

As your online community grows, it's a good idea to plan your interactions. Here are some things that I have found useful to consider as admin of our Facebook group.

DON'T POST TOO MUCH

I tend to post two to three times a week, so the group is alive and engaging, and things are happening for my followers. I schedule these posts several weeks (sometimes months) in advance, so I can batch the posting process. I take an hour once a month and get it all scheduled. Sometimes I post or share between these scheduled posts when I see or think of something that could be valuable for my group. You don't have to sit and post all day long.

POST THINGS THAT MAKE PEOPLE ENGAGE

Here are some things you can post that will make members engage with you and each other:

- Ask questions (in the language you teach): 'What did you have for breakfast?' or 'What is your favourite film and why?' Questions like these will offer members a chance to practise reading comprehension and writing in an everyday setting. Offer feedback by commenting on their answers in a friendly tone and explain any grammar or spelling that they got wrong.

- Create polls where you write a sentence and leave one word out, and then offer three options for the missing words, which they can vote for. This is great for offering grammar or vocabulary training by giving them multiple choices. Also offer explanations after a day or so in a comment, if needed.

- Posts that begin with 'Did you know...' or 'Remember...' (and include interesting cultural information or grammatical tips and tricks) are also very welcome in groups, I have found.

In *The Language Teacher Rebel Toolkit*, you'll find a cheat sheet with ideas for post themes on social media.

FOSTER A COMMUNITY WHERE MEMBERS POST AND COMMENT

Ultimately, a group should be a community and not a teacher–student environment. You should encourage members to be active and ask questions. When members ask questions, allow others to comment before jumping in to answer. Always 'like' when someone posts something. Also 'like' any answers or comments that people post. This makes members feel recognized and valued.

CREATE GROUND RULES

It's useful to create some ground rules for your group (you can include them in the group description). These can include some dos and don'ts. For example, you can encourage your members to post and ask questions but discourage them from posting spam or things that don't relate to the purpose of the group.

How to overcome insecurities on social media

We all have moments of insecurity when posting things on social media. Very few people feel completely in their element when they record themselves on camera, for example. I was incredibly nervous when launching my first online course, even though I had been teaching live for more than ten years.

But remember this; it's not really about you. It's about giving and sharing things that people actually need to hear and see. You are giving, not performing. And if you allow your insecurities to get in the way of sharing your knowledge, it means people who really need to hear it can't do so.

Of course, there are lots of things you can do to make your content look pretty, and sometimes it can be a good idea. But too 'pretty' can make it look staged and inauthentic, and your posts can start looking like ads. So focus more on giving and helping.

✖ Keeping your email list warm (but not 'spammy')

As you already know by now, your email list is one of the core features of your business. You are constantly striving to lead people towards subscribing to your email list. Therefore, it's important to also keep it warm. This can be a delicate balance to maintain. I sometimes sign up to email lists when they offer something I want (a download, for example), and then I literally get bombarded with emails afterwards.

You need to think about how you would like to use your email list. If you are blogging for your website, you can use your email list to share new blog posts.

You can also use your email list instead of a blog, if you don't like the idea of blogging (more about pros and cons of blogging in Chapter 9). You could have an opt-in on your website that says something along the lines of 'Sign up to my newsletter, you'll get exclusive content to your email.' In order for anyone to get access to the free content that you create and share, they need to sign up.

Or you can use it to occasionally send out news (new offers, for example) that you want people to know about. Or just to share something that you think your followers would find valuable.

In my *Language Teacher Rebel Toolkit*, I have provided a large selection of email scripts that you can use for your email list. You can just copy and paste them directly into an email, and add your own personal details. I've also included over 170 different subject lines for emails that engage and make followers curious, so you don't have to think of a subject line from scratch.

Repurpose your content

Avoid becoming a content-making factory. If you are constantly writing new content for your blog and your newsletter, you will soon burn out. Try to repurpose any new material you create. Squeeze as much as you can from each piece of content that you produce. It's not repetitive, and many people will actually miss your posts the first time around.

Plan your content creation so you only create the main piece once and can easily tweak it to publish in different formats on different platforms. For example, you could write a blog post and record yourself on video chatting through it. You can publish the blog post, edit the video, extract the audio from the video in a separate file, and extract short video clips from the video. Now you have one blog post (for website and email list), one video (that could be uploaded to YouTube, Facebook, Instagram, etc.), audio that could become a podcast episode, short video clips for TikTok, Twitter or Instagram reels/stories, and you can also create picture posts (for Instagram, for example) with quotes from the blog post. This is a time-saving strategy so you can get the most out of your content. But it's also a smart safeguarding strategy, in case the platforms change in the future and you need to switch platforms.

Also, remember that you can post similar things several times. Just because you've posted about one topic, it doesn't mean you can never post about it again. You can post the same quotes but with a different design. You can even repost something you've already posted. Can you remember what someone posted a year or so ago? Probably not.

✖ Gather reviews

Once you have taught some students online, you need to start gathering reviews from your students. Reviews are incredibly powerful social proof that what you do is valuable to others.

We're in a time period where traditional advertising doesn't really work for smaller businesses. We now record our TV shows so we can fast-forward through any adverts, and we pay for platforms such as Netflix and Spotify to watch films and listen to music without ads. We also buy products and services based on recommendations (by word of mouth, reviews or things we see shared by people we know on the internet and on social media) and also sometimes based on what we perceive as being good for the wider community and the planet (even if they're more expensive).

The only thing we trust today is human impressions. It's the only thing that matters. Clearly this is not a new idea. We know that we make our purchasing decisions based on emotions and relationships, from people that we know, like and trust.

If you have a website, you should set up a page where you can publish reviews. You should also show a couple of reviews on your homepage, as well as link to your reviews page from your homepage, so people can easily find it. Go to your website builder and follow the instructions on how to add a new page.

There are many ways to gather reviews, but what I do is to simply send an email to a student when they have worked with me for a while and ask them to write a review. Then I copy and paste it into my reviews page on my website. In my *Language Teacher Rebel Toolkit*, I have an email template you can use to ask for testimonials via email.

If I receive an email with some kind words, I take a screenshot of it and blur out any personal details (name, email address, etc.) to make it anonymous, and then post it on my reviews page (and perhaps share it on social media too). If someone posts something on social media about me or my lessons or courses, I share it on my social media channels.

Make it a priority to regularly gather reviews and make sure to share them so your potential students can see them.

Summary

ACTION PLAN

- Get familiar and start playing with tools for creating videos and visual content.
- Schedule posts for social media, and foster a community where members are encouraged to participate and interact.
- Think about how you want to use your email list in order to keep it warm.
- Gather reviews and publish them.

9

Developing and Investing

You have now set up your tools and shared some materials about yourself and your niche. You have some money coming in from your teaching business. While there are many things you could invest in at this stage, in this chapter I'll focus on the two elements that I think are the most important: a booking system and a website.

Booking system

Unless you really want to schedule manually in your diary, I would highly recommend investing in a booking system. You may already have one, but if you don't, or if you've only tried a free version, now would be the time to invest in a paid plan. You can embed the booking system in your website (more about websites below), or if you don't have a website, keep it separate and just use a link to share your booking system on social media channels.

Why you should have a booking system:

- To allow your students to browse your availability and choose the times that they want, and also to cancel and reschedule without having to bother you about it.

- To cut down on emailing time between you and your students. Emailing makes us feel as if we are working, but you have to remember that this is actually **unpaid work**.

- To allow you to plan your time better. You can block future dates when you don't want to/can't teach.

- To allow you to take payments in advance and have a system that takes care of your cancellation policy automatically.

I have tried a few different booking systems throughout my teaching journey, and my favourite to date is a system called Acuity Scheduling. I pay a monthly fee for one of their plans. I love it (and I am not getting paid to tell you this).

Here are the reasons why:

- It's so easy to use. Honestly.

- They allow you to block out time between appointments (so you could, for example, offer 50-minute lessons, e.g. 10.00–10.50, so you can have a quick break in-between.

- They offer packages. This was one of the major reasons why I switched to them. I sell a lot of packages of ten lessons (for a discounted price), and it's really easy to set up.

- They allow for Intake Forms, so you can ask your students some questions when they book their first lesson (for example, what level they are at, what their Skype ID is, and other relevant information).

- Their system for sending out automatic email reminders before lessons is seamless.

- Their time-zone feature is great too, so your students can book in their own time zone but it will show the times in your time zone for you.

- Their support is just fabulous, and fun.

There is also a free version and a lower-cost version, but these don't include the option to create packages. There are many other booking systems out there, but when you start looking around, make sure you don't get stuck in 'research mode'. With that, I mean don't get stuck comparing reviews of different systems. Most of them have similar features and they are all very competitive in price. Just pick one, and you'll be fine. You can always change later!

Websites

In order to create a space for yourself online, you should consider having your own website. You're building your own home on your own plot. This communicates to other people that you're real and that what you do is real.

Things to invest in:

- Domain name
- Host

The domain name is the name of your website – www. blablabla.com, for example. You'll need to buy this and you usually pay for one or two years at a time (sometimes longer). .com domain names are usually more expensive, but not necessarily required.

Thinking about what your domain name should be can feel overwhelming at first. You can end up experiencing a bit of a conflict over whether to keep it very broad, or make it very specific. The advantage of keeping it broader is that your website can accommodate slight changes to your offers or interests further down the line. A website called germanprepositionsexpert.com can become very limiting if you choose to venture outside of that micro-niche some day. You can actually use your own name as your domain, if you want to. The disadvantage is that, well, it can be too general. Having a website with a domain name that reflects your micro-niche can be very powerful.

One compromise is to use your name as your first website, but purchase additional domain names that reflect your micro-niche and have them point to your main website to start with. You might end up developing several websites later, but this can be a good start. Or, if you feel you have nailed down your micro-niche and have a really good name for it, then go for it. But purchase your name as a domain too, and let it point towards your other website.

You also need a host. This is a service that creates a space for your website on the internet. You pay, usually upfront, for this, and can generally pay on a monthly or yearly basis. There are lots of different hosts to choose from. At the time of writing this book, some of the most popular ones are WordPress, Wix, Squarespace and Weebly. I have one WordPress site and one Wix site, myself. I have to say that the Wix site is incredibly easy to get started with, so if you're new to setting up a website, this might be a good option. But most hosts nowadays come with nice-looking templates where you can drag and drop images, text and multimedia, so don't get too bogged down when you choose your host.

Most hosts allow you to buy or register a domain name from them, and an easy solution is buying your domain name and host package from the same place. You can also buy your domain names somewhere else (places like GoDaddy or 123Reg, for example). When you buy your domain name, the company you buy it from may have limitations on domain transfers (such as no transfer until 60 days after purchase, or they may charge you a fee). This is why it can be useful to buy it from the same place as your host. Another way around this is to 'point' your domain bought from one company to your website somewhere else. For example, you might have a website built with a host, but you've got your domain name with 123Reg and you can't move it for 60 days. You can still set up your domain name with 123Reg to automatically redirect to your website. So when you type in that domain name or click on a link, you'll end up on your website.

One more thing you should do is check that you get an SSL certificate. An SSL certificate means that your website will begin 'https' instead of just 'http'. It's a more secure form of http, which means your website is less vulnerable to attacks like hacking or illicit surveillance. Not only is it in your interest to keep your website safe, but it also looks professional to visitors. Many http sites now show a message saying that they're not secure, which does not look good. Some hosts include an SSL certificate in their hosting package, and others have it as an optional extra.

Designing a website is a fun and creative process, and you can of course have whatever you want on your website. I would absolutely recommend that you create your own website, unless you really don't want to. This allows you to be in full control of anything you do, what you post and design, and you don't have to ask and pay for a web designer to update it for you.

When you design your website, it's generally best to keep things simple to start with. Think about your branding and what image you want to project. Choose a minimalistic website template and work with a few colours only (one main colour and a couple that complement the main colour – these are usually built into the templates already available). There are some essential elements that you should make sure you include on your website, and these are described below.

ESSENTIAL ELEMENT 1 – HOMEPAGE

This might sound very obvious; of course every website needs a homepage. But have you really considered how important this particular page is? A lot of people only spend a couple of seconds on a homepage before they browse away from it. They only have a matter of seconds, literally, to make up their mind about you and what you do. If you pique their interest, they may stay a little longer and start to realize just how awesome and clever you are. But first impressions matter. They really do.

So what should be on your homepage? Your CV, your experience, how long you've been teaching for, what you have to offer, right?

Now is the time to take a step back and remember the lessons you learned earlier in the book. Begin with your Why statement and your Culture Add. This is what your homepage should clearly communicate. People buy with their hearts, not with their minds. We later use our minds to try and rationalize our hearts' decisions. Clearly communicate your statement that you came up with in Chapter 4 and let that lead you.

It's also nice to include a picture of yourself on the homepage. Let it be a personal and fun picture, rather than a professional-looking one.

Another super-important element for your home/first page is a sign-up option to your email list, ideally through inviting people to download your Lead Magnet.

These two elements are the most important ones for a homepage: something that communicates your Why statement and Culture Add, and a way for people to subscribe to your email list. Anything else is optional.

ESSENTIAL ELEMENT 2 – ABOUT PAGE

This is where you can talk about your background, your experience, how many hours you have taught, any educational details that are relevant, and so on. Some students like to read things like 'qualified' and 'native', but if these don't apply to you, don't worry; you can hone in on your experience. Just talk about what you have done and what you can help with. A picture is also nice to have here.

It's very useful to include a video of you talking about yourself and what you're passionate about. It doesn't have to be a long video; one or two minutes is totally fine. But it's a great way to show what you're like 'in person', so that people can get a sense of you and feel like they are connecting with you. You might also opt to show this video on your homepage. If you have a smartphone, or can borrow one, that will be enough to shoot a video on. You do not have to buy any extra equipment for this.

Here are some basic things to think about when you record:

- Lighting: natural light is great, so if you can sit or stand in a room with natural light – in front of a window in daytime, for example – that will improve your video.

- Background: make sure the background is clutter-free. It doesn't have to be perfect, but piles of clothes or dirty dishes do not look great. If you want to create a simple backdrop, you can just hang up a white or lightly coloured single sheet or duvet over a door and stand in front of it. I recorded a whole vowel pronunciation series with a cream-coloured duvet as a background. Many video-conferencing platforms also allow you to use a photo as a virtual background if you want.

- Don't worry too much about your hair, etc., you'll be surprised how much people appreciate authenticity! However, it's good to look presentable.

If you want to edit your video, there are loads of ways to do this. I have a MacBook and I have used the free iMovie program that comes with it, but there are also phone apps that you can use to download and edit your video. Just search for 'best video-editing apps for mobile' and check them out. Another great free option for a laptop is DaVinci Resolve.

ESSENTIAL ELEMENT 3 – CONTACT PAGE

Have a separate page with an option to contact you. You can just put your email address here but be aware it might mean you get some spam emails. A better option is to include some kind of contact form, where people can fill in their details and you'll receive their message in an email.

ESSENTIAL ELEMENT 4 – FAQ

These are the same FAQ that you created as one of your essential general articles in Chapter 7. Some prospective students might read them, and a lot of people won't. But you can still link to them from other pages on your website, and also in your auto-reply emails.

The FAQ should obviously contain frequently asked questions, and if you have had enquiries before, you probably know what these questions tend to be. Here are some common ones from my own experience:

- How can I book lessons with you?
- What days and hours do you teach?
- How long does it take to learn [the language you're teaching]?
- How often should I have lessons?
- What materials (if any) should I get?
- My company will pay for my lessons. How can I pay and can I get a receipt?

Think about other questions that people tend to ask, or if there are any particular aspects that you would like to highlight and note them down. Put them on the FAQ page with the question as a title and the answer underneath. You can also insert links to other pages on your website (for example, a link to your booking system page). Include a link to your email list, to encourage people to subscribe. It can be nice to use videos here too, in addition to the written text. Some people like reading, others like watching, so it's good to try and cater for as many different learning styles as possible. If you want to make a text-based video (rather than have you as a talking head), you can use something like Lumen5 to create this.

That's it; these are all your essential elements for your teaching website. If this is all you do, and you market it in a clever way, you will be on the right track!

There are a few other things that you might want to consider, so let's look at some 'nice to have' elements.

NICE TO HAVE ELEMENT 1 – BLOG

To blog or not to blog, that is the question.

Pros:

- You can show off your skills (you can, for example, blog about culture, specific language points that your students find difficult, study techniques, etc.).

- You can give prospective students a sense of how you communicate before they take the plunge and buy lessons from you.

- You'll assert yourself as an expert in your field.

- You create something that people can share.

- You can create content upgrades to encourage people to sign up to your email list.

- It will make your website look alive, rather than static.

- You can connect the publishing of blog posts to other social media platforms (so they automatically publish on Facebook, for example) and you can set up your email list system so it emails your list when you have published a new blog post. There are lots of nifty automations you can do.

- You can also reuse this content in many ways. You can create a video, you can tweet smaller sections of the blog post, you can record yourself reading it and create a podcast or a downloadable audio track.

- It's useful if you want to be found online (it's good for Search Engine Optimization).

Cons:

- It does take time.
- It takes a bit of planning.

- Some argue that it's good to blog consistently (as the website can look abandoned otherwise). You don't have to blog every week; you could blog once a month if you want, or even less often. However, there are other ways to make a website look alive (for example, by including a social media feed on your homepage, if you regularly post on social media).

You certainly don't have to blog. There are lots of alternatives that you can try, if you don't feel comfortable with the idea of blogging:

- Podcasts or voice chat platforms
- Guest blogging on other people's blogs (to get yourself in front of someone else's audience)
- Sending a newsletter to your email list as a way to communicate
- Doing social media live sessions (for example on Facebook, Instagram or YouTube)
- Webinars
- YouTube videos.

In my view, it's actually better to write fewer and longer posts, than shorter posts more often. The aim is to try and provide as much value as you can. It's better to have four or five really valuable blog posts (the Pillar Content I mentioned earlier), rather than posting mediocre content regularly. If you write longer blog posts that people find useful, they're more likely to share them.

NICE TO HAVE ELEMENT 2 – VIDEOS

This might make you feel uncomfortable, but videos (especially of yourself) are a great way to show off your personality and help prospective students connect with you. They'll feel like they are getting to know you. The videos don't have to be perfect. In fact, I think we are in an era when we really appreciate a sense of authenticity. Too strict, too arranged and too scripted can feel staged, dull and boring.

In terms of social media, videos attract more views than text-based posts and it's predicted that videos will become the predominant way that we consume content online. So it's really worth considering them and getting used to recording videos now.

NICE TO HAVE ELEMENT 3 – LINKS TO RESOURCES

Another thing that is good to include on a website is a page with links to resources that are relevant to the language you're teaching. You're communicating that you're here to help, that you're generous, and you're also affirming your role as an expert. This means that students (current and future) will be more likely to turn to you for advice and help. You could include links to any of the following:

- National newspapers
- TV channels (and particular programmes if available)
- Radio stations (and particular programmes if available)
- Online dictionaries
- Recommended books
- Information on how to get a visa/move to a country where the language is spoken
- Universities and job sites
- Free exercises online (perhaps your own flashcard sets, or something similar)
- Music artists who sing in the language you teach.

OTHER OPTIONS

If you have some social media channels, you might want to consider embedding the feeds onto your website. This way, you can show that you're active on other channels. You may not blog regularly, but if you post somewhere else more often, this feed will make your website still look alive and active. I would recommend embedding this on the homepage/first page, so that new visitors see it immediately.

IMPROVING A WEBSITE

Here are some quick tips on how to improve a website.

Homepage

Try and put yourself in your students' shoes. What's the first impression you have as you enter your website? Is it clear who you help and what you offer? What's the feeling you get from looking at it? Do the images, colour, layout and text support your message? If you're unsure, you can always ask a friend to give you some feedback. Also, make sure there is a clear 'call to action'. Are visitors supposed to join your email list, follow you on social media, or contact you directly?

About page

This should be much more than just a dry CV. This is where potential students find out about you, what makes you tick, why you're doing what you're doing. This section should be lively, personal, but also authoritative. Take a close look at the page. Does it tell your story? Is it relevant to your audience and the services/products you're selling? Does it communicate your values, strengths, credibility and authority?

Services/Lessons page

Here is where you list what you offer. Spend a little time analysing whether it really says something about how you help people and the results people can expect. Are there testimonials from past students? How are you reassuring people that you're the right person to help them?

TEN QUICK TIPS ON HOW TO GET A WEBPAGE TO RANK HIGHER IN INTERNET SEARCHES

The most important focus is keywords. Basically, you have to match the question (the keyword and the search intent of this keyword) and the offer (your webpage). You'll need to think about this for most, if not all, of the pages on your website. You need to think about Search Engine Optimization (SEO). To start with, focus on your homepage.

1. Create a list of (search) words

Choose one very specific combination of words that best suits that question. Not one word, but a combination of descriptive words. For example, 'Modern wedding photographer Stockholm', 'Solving midlife crisis therapy for men', or 'Business French lessons online for professionals'. The more specific the question is that you answer, the greater the chance that you'll rank high. Now go back to your webpage that you want to match to these search words.

2. Make the webpage the best webpage on this specific topic in your area

Look through the text on your webpage. Is it unique? Does it read well? Is it interesting? Does it add something? Is it different from competing webpages?

Search for your keywords and view the pages of the competitors. Does your webpage have better content, and is it more attractively designed? Is the problem (and the solution) discussed and described in detail? Does the question (from the potential student) and the offer (your webpage) match perfectly? No? Don't worry. Every webpage can be improved. Go away and research for half an hour (gather extra facts, stories, quotes and figures about the problem and your solution) and then try to expand on and improve the articles on this webpage. Remember: the more specific the subject (the keywords), the easier it is to create one of the best webpages on the topic (basically, remember to stick to your micro-niche).

You now have a webpage that is stronger in terms of content. But we can still optimize it further. Consider this question: can the searcher immediately see that you can help him or her further? Of course you can help, but can they see this? A precondition for ranking high in Google, for example, is that the webpage has to be very relevant to the search (the keywords that a searcher uses). The searcher must be able to see quickly and clearly that you can best solve his or her problem.

3. Give your text a strong title

When you publish a page or a blog post, you can give it two titles – one for the search engine (which is shown in the search results) and one that is seen on the page itself. Sometimes the normal title is already suitable for SEO, but sometimes it's smarter to write a title especially for the search engine. This is called an SEO title. Just google your website host and the words SEO title (for example, 'Wix SEO title', or 'WordPress SEO title') for more information about where to insert your SEO titles.

To create a strong SEO title, make sure it contains the search term combination that you want the page to rank for.

So rather than, say, 'Russian – lessons – Zoom', it's better to have 'C1 Russian lessons via Zoom'.

4. Create a catchy introduction

Most people are lazy readers. We skim read, glance, and dart back and forth over text. But almost everyone reads introductions. An introduction should briefly and powerfully summarize the whole article. It should reassure the reader and show them how you can help. You do this by describing their problem. A nice way to start is with a little story that the reader can identify with. In the second paragraph you link the story with your article. Then try to include the keywords in the first or second paragraph of your text.

5. Pay attention to the headings

Headings function as stop signs for online text. They help readers to focus on key information. If you have more headings, you have more attention from a reader. So make sure you have several headings and not just long paragraphs of text.

6. Use white space

The more white space you use, the better your text is understood. It gives a text an impression of air and lightness, even if it means the text will be physically longer. And avoid overly long sentences, as they are also more difficult to read.

7. Make your webpage attractive

You can use text to convey a message, but there are many other aspects that create an impression and communicate an idea. Consider your style and branding – the font, colours, images and maybe also videos, as they can all make your website more visibly attractive.

8. Create links

You should link to other pages from your pages. These could be to other articles on your website, but links should also be to other external, quality websites that are relevant to your page. You can find out which pages are relevant (according to a search engine) by putting the keywords into that search engine and seeing what comes up.

9. Make sure it's mobile-friendly

When a website shows up on a mobile phone in a mobile-friendly way, it's not displayed as on a desktop site. Your website might already have this function built into its template, or you can use a plugin if necessary. Either way, make sure it displays as a mobile site on a mobile phone. Search engines like this.

10. Make your website https

As I mentioned earlier, SSL certificates enable https websites (a secure form of http). Search engines like https websites. If you don't already have https, you can check with your website host if they have https certificates. Some include this in their price, others have it as an optional extra. Either way, you should make sure you have it.

If you have followed these steps, you'll have more powerful webpages that will rank higher in search engines such as Google. If you have updated a webpage, you can share it again on your social media channels. If it's a blog post, you can change the date to today and place it at the top of your blog page (and share again).

Online business platforms

At this point you may want to explore whether you would be better off investing in a complete online business platform (such as Kajabi or Kartra). These platforms require monthly or yearly payment and usually cost more than £100/ $100 per month. Therefore, you need to be sure that you're consistently bringing in enough income to spend this kind of money. The upside is that online business platforms combine many of the other programs that you would be using and perhaps paying for. They include things like an email list program, a booking system, an online course delivery program, a website, payment processing, and some also have community/forum features. But this all depends on what type of services and/or products you want to focus on, and what your revenue is like. There is also a risk with putting everything onto one platform. On the one hand, it can be very handy to have everything in one place. On the other hand, if anything happens with this particular platform, you could become very vulnerable.

Summary

ACTION PLAN

- Upgrade to a paid plan on your online booking system, if you haven't already.
- Develop your website.
- Consider whether you want to have a blog.
- Optimize your website to make it easier for search engines to find it.

10

Flourish with Momentum

So, you have taken the step to become a Language Teacher Rebel, found your micro-niche and started teaching students online. You have set up some tools and created content that has led to your students finding you. You are enjoying the freedom of working for yourself in a geographically flexible environment, the opportunities for creative output and engaging with different people from different countries. What's next?

In this chapter, I'll go through some things that you might want to consider in order to grow your business and expand as a Language Teacher Rebel. I'll focus on three main aspects: making videos and going live, developing partnerships, and creating systems to free up more time. At the end of the chapter, I'll also touch upon some typical challenges that you might encounter on the way: having too many or too few bookings, how to increase your prices, how to outsource, and how to 'break up' with a student.

Making videos and going live

If the idea of recording videos and streaming live videos fills you with dread, you are not alone! I have felt so uncomfortable and nervous when it comes to being on camera, but it does get easier with time and practice.

Of course, you don't have to be on video in order to run an online teaching business. However, it's worth considering it for these reasons:

- It's a great way to show your students who you are. We connect more with videos than with text or still photos. You create a more intimate and personal atmosphere, which will build trust in you and what you do.

- If you have a Facebook page/group, you should know that the Facebook algorithm heavily favours videos and live streams (this is also true for Instagram). Facebook doesn't like you sharing YouTube videos though (YouTube is a competitor), so make sure you share original content. You can upload the same video to YouTube as well, but it's best not to post YouTube links in your Facebook account. If you do this, just be aware that they will usually get fewer views.

- There are recent studies predicting that over 75 per cent of internet traffic will be videos within a couple of years from now. Whether that turns out to be true or not, we can predict that video content will continue to grow in popularity, so it's good to get used to it now!

PRE-RECORDED VIDEOS

You can record, edit and publish videos on your website and on any social media channels. You can record them on a smartphone or with a camera on your laptop. I have recorded almost all my videos on my smartphone, and then edited them on my laptop (if I felt they needed editing).

You can record videos of yourself just talking into the camera ('talking head') or you can create slides (in PowerPoint or Google Slides) where you talk over your slides. Good examples of programs for recording these types of videos are Loom, Zoom and ScreenFlow.

There are so many things you can do with videos, but here are some ideas to get you started:

- Pronunciation videos (demonstrating in detail how to pronounce letters, specific words and phrases)
- Grammar videos (explaining particular grammatical issues)
- 'How-to' videos (showing how to order a coffee or ask for directions, for example)
- Culture videos (explaining culture-related points)
- Behind the scenes (showing your office, your surroundings, you at work and your daily routines/tools, for example).

If your students agree, you can also record yourself teaching a lesson online. This is very powerful content to create, as you will be showing exactly how you teach someone. You don't have to publish the whole lesson, but you can use snippets of the lesson in many different contexts to show how you work.

LIVE STREAMS

On many social media platforms, you have the option to live stream. This means you 'go live', talking directly to your audience through live-streamed video. Consider inviting special guests from your field to discuss particular points relevant to your language or culture.

Before you go live to your audience, you can practise by doing a private broadcast (which means only you can see it), so you can test your sound, lighting, and so on. It's good to plan ahead; you can make notes on specific points that you want to talk about. However, it's a lot more casual and relaxed than live TV. Make sure you have no major distractions and a good broadband connection. Ideally, use your laptop or a mobile phone on a tripod, so the video doesn't appear shaky.

Tell people when you are going to go live ahead of time. If you are doing a live social media session, you can make a post/story about it, and you could also set it up as an 'event' so people can bookmark it.

It's more engaging for your viewers to make a live stream interactive. Greet viewers by name as they enter the live stream, ask questions and encourage viewers to type responses, and then respond to their questions. Also remember that not everyone starts watching at the same time, so it's good to briefly remind people later during the live stream what it is that you are doing ('for those who have just joined, welcome…, we're currently talking about…, and we've just covered…').

You can always search for tips for live streaming; there are lots of good video examples you can watch to get some inspiration.

Developing partnerships

Let's start by exploring why you should develop partnerships. Besides the fact that it's fun and inspiring to work with others, it's also the fastest way to grow your business. You should identify other people in your industry who could complement your micro-niche and who already have an audience or community.

The intention is for you to be introduced to that community by their leader. Not only will you get in front of new people (a bit like when you guest post, which I talked about in the previous chapter), but being introduced by the leader of that community will also build a large amount of trust in you. The community members (or the audience) already trust the leader of that community, and if this person introduces you to them, you are not just coming in from the cold, so to speak. It's like a friend introducing one of their friends to you, compared to a salesperson you have never met before knocking on your door, trying to sell you something.

It is important that any collaborators should not be your competitors. They should not be doing exactly the same thing as you. Instead, they should offer something else to the same audience that you are interested in. Another word for this is *vertical market partner*. Let's say that you are teaching Japanese to English expats. Vertical market partners could have a blog, a podcast or a video channel for English expats in Japan. This could be about how to find a house, meet other expats, or declare your taxes in Japan. Or your vertical market partner could have a magazine that publishes articles for expats in Japan. They are not offering any language services (or at least not within your micro-niche) but they already have a large audience within the English expat community. They serve the same customers, but in a different way. By partnering up with someone like this, you can complement each other with what you offer to this audience. Spend some time researching who could be your potential vertical market partners.

THE FOUR-WEEK COURTING METHOD

Once you have found some possible partners, it's time to network. Here's what you should not do: send an email out of the blue to this person, asking if you can collaborate. Instead, you need to build up the relationship over a period of time.

Of course, you can take as long as you want to build a relationship, but let's look at how you could do this in a four-week period. The structure of this four-week process comes from Mariah Coz and the *Mariah Coz Show* podcast.

Before exploring what a four-week 'courting period' could look like, make sure you go into this with the right frame of mind. The person you are trying to connect with may just ignore you. Or turn you down in the end. This is totally ok. Don't automatically expect that they will reciprocate. You shouldn't feel like they owe you something, just because you have spent time getting to know them and built a relationship. It might not be the right time. They may come back to you later instead. Or it might not be a good fit for them. And that's fine too. Don't feel like you're entitled to their attention or feel bitter because they have turned you down. It may turn into a partnership, or it may not. Or it may become one at a later stage. Just keep going.

During your first week, you need to identify all your potential collaborators in your niche. You can do this in a document or in a spreadsheet. Write down their name, their website and social media channels, the size of their audience (followers, group members, etc.) and what they do. Don't be afraid to put 'big' names on this list! You are going to build your confidence along the way and work your way up to those bigger names.

If you don't know who these people are already, do a thorough search on Google, Facebook, Instagram, Twitter, YouTube, and all the other platforms that you can think of. When you find someone who looks like a good fit, go one step further and explore who *they* follow. This will take some time, but eventually you are going to have a list of 50+ potential collaborators.

In the second week, you need to go through your list of people and subscribe to their newsletters and follow them on any social media platforms that they are active on. During this stage, you need to really keep an eye on what they are doing. Look at their posts, read their newsletters, watch their videos, listen to their podcasts. You can also start liking their posts, maybe leave a comment, and perhaps also repost something of theirs. When you start liking their posts, you start to come up on their radar. They will start to notice you.

This stage is important, because later when you start making more direct contact, you can refer to what they are doing and show that you are up-to-date on their work. If you contact someone and ask them what they are working on at the moment, and they have just uploaded a lot of posts about their new service or product on social media, you can come across as uninformed and you'll have missed an opportunity to make a good first impression. This is also an opportunity for you to find out more about them, in order to establish whether you think they are a good fit for you. You might realize that you don't like their way of working, and cross them off your list. So do not skip this step.

During week 3, you'll start to make direct contact with the person. You can do this by commenting directly to them or replying directly to one of their posts. In week 3, you'll also start sharing their content on your platforms. You can share their posts on social media, write a comment about why you find them really useful and tag them in it. When you tag them in your post, they will see that you have shared their content to your followers. You may even dedicate a whole blog post to them and what you have learned from them (and link to their website or platform).

The keywords for this week are generosity and giving. You'll want to make a good impression and show what you're about. Remember that they still may not reciprocate, and that's completely fine.

In week 4, you're going to establish direct contact with them. The easiest way to do this is to reply to one of their newsletters. Tell them how much you liked the content that they shared, tell them what you have learned from them, and so on. Don't fake it; be specific and complement them on something that you genuinely found interesting, helpful or inspiring. This is where what you have been doing in weeks 2 and 3 comes in, because if you have been following them and you know what they are up to, you can say something about that too.

If you can in some way demonstrate how what they have done has impacted you, or led to a positive result for you, then make sure to mention this too. This can lead to them being more interested in featuring you on their platforms. What you are trying to do here is to open up a direct, private channel of communication with them. If they do respond to you, this is an opportunity (if you want) to mention the possibility of some kind of future collaboration, and if you can, try and offer something in return.

If you have gone through this process and don't get a response, don't worry. Keep engaging on social media, keep sharing and keep an eye on what they do. As mentioned before, people may be busy and it may not be the right time. So keep being generous and keep giving. Let the whole process of relationship building be a part of your business moving forward.

OUTSOURCING

When you hear the word 'outsourcing' your first thought is probably of call centres in a different country. What outsourcing really means is allocating certain tasks to someone else. That someone could be a specific professional or a virtual assistant for more general admin tasks. For example, you might want to engage a designer to design a logo, an editor to edit a podcast episode, a transcriber to transcribe interviews, someone who can create captions for your social media videos, or a social media manager to take care of your social media accounts. Many people also outsource managing their financial accounts, especially if they have to pay VAT/sales tax.

Outsourcing can free you up from easy or repetitive tasks, so that you can focus on creating more new products. Or it can help you with something you are not very good at or that needs a professional touch. This means that you can concentrate on tasks that will create more value in your business.

Here are three questions you should consider:

- What are some of the tasks that you have to do every week that you find boring and repetitive?
- What are some of the tasks that you have to do, but that you find difficult and take a long time?
- What are some things you would love to do/have, but don't have the necessary technical skills to create?

You don't have to hire someone full-time, but you could consider hiring someone for a few hours here and there to do things that you find difficult or time-consuming. Here are some tasks that you might want to consider outsourcing:

- Creating graphics (logo, social media graphics, e-books, etc.)
- Transcribing interviews or creating captions (if you are making videos)
- Scheduling blog posts, emails and social media posts
- Managing your financial accounts.

TAKING ON ANOTHER TEACHER AS A SUBCONTRACTOR/FREELANCER

If you have more students than you can cope with, you might want to consider taking on another teacher as a subcontractor. Subcontracting means you have a teacher who teaches for you, and they send you an invoice for the hours they have taught.

This step can feel scary, as you have built up your brand and someone else could do damage to it. It's therefore very important that you carefully select someone who is aligned with your values. Your co-teacher should have the same overall values and goals as you do and be passionate about the same areas. They should be able to form positive relationships with their students, so that the students want to come back to them.

Of course, they also need to know what they are doing in terms of teaching your language and be able to teach broadly in the same way as you do (however, you shouldn't be micro-managing them). If you find a person who fits the bill, it can be incredibly rewarding to have a co-teacher. You'll have a colleague who you can talk to and maybe even create new projects together with.

As you are providing your co-teacher with students, marketing of your services, a booking system, and so on, you need to pay your co-teacher less than what you charge your students. The amount that you keep (the difference between what your students pay and what your co-teacher invoices you for) should correspond to the overheads of your business.

You should also create a written agreement that your co-teacher signs. I'm not a legal professional, so you should seek legal advice, but here are some things that you might want to include in any agreement: clarification of your relationship, what happens if they want to leave, or you want to end the agreement, and also clarification that your co-teacher is not allowed to take the students you give them and teach them privately, away from your business.

Creating systems to free up time

By creating systems in your business, you will be able to free up more time for yourself. If you have gone through the steps in this book you will already have set up some automations: an autoresponder for your email, creating a Lead Magnet that helps you to grow your email list, and investing in a booking system that sends out reminders, for example. It's time to look at some other ways that you can automate and systematize your processes, so you can create more free time for yourself.

SCHEDULING SOCIAL MEDIA POSTS

If you haven't already, you should start using a social media management software package. By using this type of software, you can schedule posts in advance and let the software post them for you on several social media platforms. This means you don't have to go onto every social media platform in order to post something, which saves a lot of time.

The software I use at the moment is Buffer (there are many others, like Hootsuite, for example).

When you use social media management software, you can really put batching into practice. You can use a social media calendar to plan out all your posts and write out the captions and any hashtags (especially for Instagram, if you use it). Then, copy and paste them into your social media management system, upload the photos you want to post with them, and schedule them for the day and the time you want them to publish. When you work in this way, spend an hour or so scheduling posts in advance on multiple platforms. It's a really great and productive way to batch this type of marketing activity.

As I mentioned earlier, you can also schedule posts on Facebook (both on your page and in your group) several months in advance. Make sure you start using these features, as they will save you a lot of time in the long run.

CAPTURING PROCESSES INTO TEMPLATES

When you find that you do certain things again and again and they involve several steps, you should capture these processes into workflows and templates. Let's say, for example, you answer an email to a student about rescheduling a lesson on your booking system: you can copy and paste your answer into a document so you have the main text ready if someone else asks you the same question. This way, you don't have to compose another answer from scratch. If it's something that a lot of people ask, consider including the question and answer in your FAQ, or create a separate PDF about it, that you can refer people to.

The same is true when you find a way to do something that solves a problem for you. Maybe you have been searching for how to update something on your website, and you finally find the perfect solution. Write the steps down in a document and save it, so you can go back to it if you encounter the same issue again. Then all you have to do is follow the steps, instead of having to do the research again.

I have collected all my best business templates in my *Language Teacher Rebel Toolkit*, available at www.library.teachyourself. com. You can buy and download it, and then you can just amend them as you like and insert your own details.

ESTABLISHING WEEKLY ROUTINES

When you have a weekly routine, you don't have to wake up every morning wondering what to do. Your weekly routine can take whatever shape you want, but try and batch admin tasks as much as possible. It's much more effective spending a couple of hours on a Monday creating content and scheduling posts, than jumping back and forth between lessons throughout the whole week. When you plan to do something, make sure you block that time out so you don't get distracted; easier said than done, I know!

You should also make time every week to review both what you have done and what you are going to do. You can follow these five steps during this process:

Step 1: Review the last week

You can do this either at the beginning of the week or at the end of a week. Review what you have spent and made financially (expenses and income). You can also review your week in a more qualitative way: what went well, what needs more work, etc.

Step 2: Review 90-day goals and outcomes

There is no point planning any further ahead than 90 days. Things change and your goals will change too, but you should have a 90-day action plan. You can keep this as a working document that you come back to every week. This is an opportunity to check in and see where you are, what things need to be done, and what needs to be added, removed or modified.

Step 3: Review two-week action plan

As I mentioned in Chapter 7, a great way to break bigger projects into manageable pieces is through the Sprint Method. A sprint is always two weeks, so it's a great idea to have a two-week action plan in parallel to your 90-day goals and outcomes plan. Make sure to review this weekly too, so you know where you are in the two-week cycle and what you need to do next.

Step 4: Review calendar

Look at the week ahead in terms of student work, lessons booked, and other things you need to do for your business, but also for your private life. How does your week look?

Step 5: Plan when to do tasks and make adjustments

A useful way to plan out your tasks is to put them into your calendar. If you think 'I'll just do that when I have some spare time', chances are it won't get done at all. Now is also the time to allow for adjustments. Do you need to change anything (and if so, how might that affect your two-week action plan)? If you have too many tasks planned, you might need to reschedule some tasks, or maybe reschedule or cancel something on your calendar. Or delegate, perhaps outsourcing something to someone else, in order to get it done.

Dealing with challenges

Challenges are unavoidable. In life, and also in your business. Here are some of the most common challenges for self-employed language teachers: having too many or too few bookings, needing to raise prices, needing to 'break up' with a student, and maintaining a good work–life balance.

TOO MANY OR TOO FEW BOOKINGS

If you teach live, your bookings can fluctuate. This is normal, but it can feel very scary in the beginning. If this is the only product you offer, it can feel stressful as your income depends on it. No bookings, no money, right?

Try (as best as you can) to not go into panic mode. Instead, spend your time planning and creating content and future products. I spent several years completely panicking every December as my bookings almost halved. I was so worried and thought I would never get a fully booked day ever again. After a few years, I noticed a pattern. I had fewer bookings in December every year, as students were busy with Christmas parties and holidays. But then, without fail, I would be fully booked again in January and February. Why? The New Year's resolution cycle. A lot of people make New Year's resolutions; we all start the New Year with dreams, aspirations and plans for the future. Learning a language is one of the typical things people seem to want to start (or restart) in the new year.

Once I realized this, I started to plan my year around it. This meant that I was doing a lot of focused development work (creating new content, creating new courses, scheduling content publishing, planning, etc.) in December, so I would be ready for when the January rush came. I also started planning my content so that any blog posts or any social media content would address the people who wanted to start learning; for example, blog posts that related to my FAQ, or how to get started learning a language. I also noticed that I had a similar but smaller rush in September, when people came back to work after their summer holiday.

Bear in mind that these things can be cyclical and try and make the most of your time to create and plan products that you can sell, if you don't already have them. This way, you'll have another income stream that is not dependent on your bookings. This is an excellent opportunity to work on developing your Product Ecosystem.

If you have too many bookings, you have an almost equally stressful but somewhat nicer problem. You can put people in a queue, you can subcontract another teacher to work alongside you to take some students off your hands, or you can raise your prices.

HOW TO RAISE PRICES

Prices go up with time. This is part of the normal inflation process, and to raise your prices accordingly is quite acceptable. You can look up the current inflation rate in your country and adjust your prices to match. Or, do a benchmarking exercise (compare your price against your competitors) and raise if you find your prices are too low. Just make sure to communicate this price increase clearly and well in advance to your students.

This can feel scary as you might be fearful that it will put students off. In *The Language Teacher Rebel Toolkit*, I've included a price increase email script showing you an easy way to do this.

If you are fully booked or/and have people on a waiting list, then you should consider raising the price.

Another way around this, and I would argue, often a better approach, is to create a new offer.

New product offer

When you create a new product, this is a good time to raise your prices. If you are teaching live, you could create a product where your students send you writing exercises and record pronunciation exercises, which you then give feedback on. Or you could create an online course. Or a blended offer. If you create something new, you can't compare it to what you have done before, which gives you flexibility when setting a new price.

Less time, rather than a higher price

If you don't want to raise the price, you could cut down the time you spend teaching. For example, your lessons could be 45 minutes instead of 60 minutes long, but for the same price. You would gain 15 minutes for every hour. I have to say this can be deceptive as you may end up running over the 45 minutes. Also, I am not sure you can really use those 15 minutes for anything useful, as it's such a small amount of time. But incorporating more breaks into your day may give you a calmer workday.

Add something to increase value

You can rename your offer and add something unique to your package that gives it extra value. It's difficult to justify why people should pay a higher price for the same product, beyond the usual rise in line with inflation. You could add extra digital products (PDFs, for example, which you only need to create once), or offer a recorded version of the class. Anything that you think your students would love.

Make sure to give this product a different name. Language is a powerful tool, as we all know. When you give it a new name and a new description, the offer will feel different from your previous offers.

HOW TO 'BREAK UP' WITH A STUDENT

Most of the time, the relationship with your students will be exciting, inspiring, fun and heart-warming. But sometimes, a relationship might just not work out. You may find you are not enjoying working with a person, or feel you have nothing more to give them. I have found that if this happens, it tends to sort itself out. You'll either find a way forward to work with them, or they will simply stop booking (and you'll feel relieved that they have left). But what if you actually need to 'break up' with a student?

Start by asking yourself these three questions:

- What is causing you the most dissatisfaction working with this student and can it be fixed?

- Would you feel better if you took a break from this student?

- Does letting go of this student help you to achieve your overall goal in your business?

If you have answered no to the second half of the first question and yes to the second and third, then you need to take the next step.

Frame the communication in such a way that you are not burning any bridges. You want the student to think highly of you and still recommend you to others in the future. Here are some potential directions you can choose from, and adjust to fit your specific issue:

- I'm looking to move away from this niche and explore new opportunities.
- I have a new goal and I need to change my business model to achieve it.
- I'm taking an indefinite vacation from this kind of work.
- I'm trying to reduce my workload due to being overwhelmed.

You could also have a conversation where you tell your student that you think they would benefit from a different type of approach, and offer an alternative (for example, an intensive course somewhere else, or another teacher who specializes in something you think would benefit them).

Set a time and 'give them notice'. This is important as it gives them time to find an alternative and it gives you time to prepare for any income loss. Another way to put people off is to simply raise your price! But you might feel this is too risky, and having a dialogue with any difficult students is probably better for your credibility in the long run.

WORK–LIFE BALANCE

Finally, as you grow your business, it's also incredibly important to make sure you look after yourself. If you become overworked, you won't do a good job, so this is crucial for your success.

Here are some general things you should consider, to make the most out of your new lifestyle:

- Make sure you plan holidays and bank holidays well in advance. Block them from your calendar, so that students can't book you. Make sure to take time off. During time off, change your usual autoresponder on your email to a message that says you are on holiday and includes your return date.

- Make sure to take breaks in the day. This might seem obvious, but when you work on your own and get absorbed by something, you can end up stuck in front of the computer for hours. And we all know that's not a good thing. Take a walk, do a ten-minute yoga break to stretch out your back, neck and the rest of your body (there are lots of free videos online you can use). Or take a nap.

- If you feel overwhelmed by the things you need to do, sit down and plan them out. Write them in a journal, or on a piece of paper. If you know you'll be getting stuck into an important aspect of your business on Monday, you can relax and do something else on Saturday and Sunday.

- I highly recommend blocking out several weeks from your regular activities throughout the year, so you can spend that time on something more focused. This should be in addition to any holiday you take. I have started blocking out one week every three or four months. It might be that you want to complete a sprint so you can create a course or new content, or you might need to do some more focused planning work. Or maybe you just need to rest! But the important thing is that you block these weeks off a long time in advance. You will thank yourself when you realize you have a break coming up and your students will fit in around it.

- Link up with other Language Teacher Rebels. Share your experiences and connect with other teachers who work online. For more information about the Language Teacher Rebel community, go to annelihaake.com.

Summary

ACTION PLAN

- Consider starting to record videos, if you haven't already. Practice makes perfect.
- Develop partnerships with vertical marketing partners, through a 'courting process' via social media. Don't be discouraged if a partnership is not formed immediately.
- Set up systems and processes to free up more of your time.
- Remember that bookings can be cyclical. Spend quiet periods designing and developing products and services that add to your Product Ecosystem.
- Creating a new offer is a good way to give yourself a pay rise.
- Start thinking of things you could outsource.
- Plan holidays, weeks off and daily breaks to maintain a healthy work–life balance.

11

Teaching online – Best practice

There are many ways to organize your teaching online. What you need to do depends on what type of service/product you offer. If you create online courses, you will design course material and create videos and downloadable resources. However, if you are teaching live online, there are a few things that can be useful to think about.

I have tried many different strategies, and the tips and recommendations shared in this chapter are based on what has worked for me and my experience of teaching adults online, mainly one-to-one or in pairs. I'll first share some advice on how to get your material organized, and then I'll talk about how you can profile your students using the Six Characters of Drama, and through this knowledge decide what exercises and activities to use in your teaching.

But first, let's get organized.

Organize your material

When you teach online, it's important to have all your material easily available in digital form. It's also important that you don't design every lesson uniquely for each student.

Why?

Don't reinvent the wheel. It takes too much time, and you want to minimize the time you have to spend preparing for a lesson so that you can go straight from one lesson to the next. You don't get paid for the time you don't teach.

Also, if you have only digital material, you can work from anywhere on your laptop – even if the student has the physical copies of the material. It makes your work life very flexible and is at the heart of being a Language Teacher Rebel.

Here are four things that are useful to have in your digital library:

1. FOLDERS FOR EVERY STUDENT, NAMED AFTER THEM

In this folder you can keep everything that is relevant to that student: copies of invoices, their lesson logs (we'll come to the lesson logs in a moment), homework they have sent you, material you have sent them, etc.

2. TEXTBOOKS AND WORKBOOKS

Let's face it, beginners in particular need to go through roughly the same things in order to learn a language. There's no need for you to write your own book (unless you want to, of course!); use the best ones in your field. If you don't have a textbook that you already work with, look into the most popular ones for your language. Market them on your website so that the student buys a copy. Gently guide the student through the textbook and give listening practice and exercises as homework. Next lesson, you can start by going through the homework.

Ideally, use textbooks that refer to the CEFR (Common European Framework of Reference for Languages) or ACTFL (American Council on the Teaching of Foreign Languages) levels, depending on where your student is based, so that the student gets a sense of progress. I have three main courses that I teach from: one for A1–A2, one for B1–B2, and one for B2–C1. They include a textbook, a workbook and also accompanying audio clips for listening exercises (great to give as homework as the student can do them independently and at their own pace).

3. WORKSHEETS FOR COMMON GRAMMAR ISSUES

You can design these yourself. They don't have to be super-fancy but should deal with particular language issues. For example, in Swedish, many students struggle with word order, so I have made a cheat sheet for this. When we come to this point in the textbook, I give them a copy of this document and talk them through it. Think through what areas are particularly tricky for your students and create some additional material for them. You can also use these cheat sheets or templates to make content upgrades and write blog posts to attract new students. Create them however you want (in Word, PowerPoint/Google Slides or even Canva).

4. OTHER RESOURCES, FILED BY TOPIC

There may be other books that you want to use, besides a textbook and a workbook. Make sure to have digital copies of these too. You may find other useful resources, such as articles that are good for discussions, quizzes or pictures. When you find new materials, or use something new during a lesson, make sure to save it into this folder.

WHERE TO KEEP YOUR DIGITAL LIBRARY

You should keep these documents somewhere you can reach them online, so somewhere in the cloud (using services like

Google Drive or Dropbox, for example). If I had to teach from someone else's computer, I could still get to all my personal documents by logging on to my account on the internet. I also use it every day as a tool for sharing files with my students, by giving them a link that they can use to view or download a file.

LESSON LOGS

A lesson log is a personalized document in which you keep track of when and what you have covered with each of your students. There are many different ways to do this, but the most important thing is that you keep track of your students. It's important to note down the date you taught them, what you did during the lesson (roughly, or maybe just which page you finished on in the textbook), what homework (if any) you have given them, and any other additional notes that might be useful (e.g. what you talked about covering in the next lesson).

This way, you can simply open the lesson log a couple of minutes before the lesson starts, and immediately be up to date with where you left off in the previous lesson with this student. You can immediately see what homework you gave, and so on.

I always try to take down some personal notes about the student (where they are from, why they are learning, what they do for a living, maybe their partner's name (especially if they are a native speaker of the language), so I can easily refer back to this information during any session.

Six Characters of Drama – understanding your students' mindsets

Students are all individuals. They have their own backgrounds, habits, strengths, weaknesses and challenges. When you meet and teach your students, you will encounter (or get a sense of) the voices in their heads. Yes, we all have voices in our heads. We can call them voices, attitudes, archetypes or characters. But we all have them.

Before looking at different student characters and what their typical behaviours, struggles and needs might be, first let me briefly go through these voices/characters, inspired by the 'Six Characters of Drama' (from the book *MindWorks* by Gary van Warmerdam - note I have used some different character names here).

The Judge

The Judge is one of the big characters in many of our heads. The Judge is always comparing. We are either 'worse than' or 'better than', or something we do is 'worse than' or 'better than'. The Judge compares us to a standard that we have set up in our imagination.

If a student's Judge tells them they're 'worse than', they may believe that they are not good enough, that what they have done doesn't measure up. They can end up being very harsh on themselves for not understanding something, or not being able to do something. The Judge tells them that they 'should know better', or 'be better by now'. This can be quite demoralizing. It may also compare them to, for example, native speakers. Which is quite an unfair comparison!

If the Judge tells them they're 'better than', it can inflate their ego and tell them that they're very good, when in fact they may need to work on a few things. This can lead to taking a course that is too high for their level, for example, or not paying attention when the teacher tells them that they need to practise more.

The Victim

The Victim often goes hand in hand with the Judge. The Victim receives judgment from the Judge and agrees with it. It's like you have one voice talking in your head that says: 'I did not remember this'. But what is implied is 'I should have remembered it.' The Victim confirms: 'I didn't remember it, I failed'.

The Victim attitude is one of hopelessness and powerlessness. The Victim is also characterized by a lot of blame. One of the primary emotions that you will find with victimhood is fear. It's the fear of not knowing, not being in control, not being safe.

A Victim attitude may lead a student to be fearful and try to avoid the feeling of not knowing and not being in control. Of course, whenever we're learning something new, it's impossible to avoid a feeling of not knowing. It comes as part and parcel of the process. But the Victim character may feel very uncomfortable in this situation. It may trigger uncomfortable emotions or memories from their school years, when they felt out of control, or when they didn't know something.

The Villain

This character can take a couple of different forms. It can be in the shape of a Rebel ('don't tell me what to do'). It can also be in the shape of a Saboteur. This side of the Villain has a tendency to sabotage their own wellbeing. The Saboteur character can be prepared to throw a whole relationship away, just because of a minor incident. But it can also damage and destroy by neglect. It can talk the student into not doing things they need to do, so they procrastinate and let things slip.

The Saboteur is the character that most often rears its head in language learning. Procrastinating, postponing, not keeping up a study routine, not doing the homework. Finally it will tell a student that there is no point in continuing. Then perhaps the Judge in their head tells them that they have failed, and the Victim agrees. And so they stop studying all together. It's easy to see how these three characters work together and collude, and they can really make a language-learning journey difficult.

The Hero

The Hero character is one that wants to help others, but they can also be driven by a deep need for admiration, praise and attention. They want to prove themselves worthy. They perform, while the crowds cheer and they receive attention. They receive praise and they get *noticed*.

When learning a language, a Hero character may lie behind frantic studying to get the best grades or test results. Their motivation may be based on external aspects; what people around them think of them. Even though external motivation may be powerful in certain circumstances, it can lead to a situation where someone is learning even though they aren't actually enjoying it. And while it may see someone through preparing for a language level test, it's much better in the long run to nurture a student's internal motivation. Internal motivation is enjoyment. It's the satisfaction of making progress, enjoying the learning journey, feeling curious and open, feeling satisfied when understanding something tricky.

The Entitled

The main attitude of the Entitled is, of course, entitlement. The Entitled feels that they deserve and are owed something. Criteria are expected to be met, and standards upheld. Entitled characters take things for granted, and feel puzzled, and maybe even angry when they do not receive what they feel they're entitled to.

Learning a new language can be difficult for the Entitled, as they may feel entitled to results and achievement, but may not realize they need to put in the hard work for themselves. They may feel that simply by taking part in a language course, the results should just materialize. After all, they have paid for it, right?

The Self-Sacrificer

This character sacrifices their wellbeing and emotional happiness for very small gain. A Self-Sacrificer can be a workaholic, who works so hard that they sacrifice their friendships, family life, and/or physical wellbeing. They may sacrifice their own wellbeing to please someone else and get their approval.

A Self-Sacrificer character may lead a student to study frantically too, just like the Hero. Perhaps they are trying to please someone in particular (parents, partner, etc.). They may study verb forms until their eyes are sore, almost as if it were a punishment.

Seven Student Characters

Now that you've got a sense of how these characters may operate, let me introduce you to seven Student Characters that I regularly encounter. These are not the only ones, and there are certainly combinations of these too. But these are the most common characters that I meet every week as a language teacher.

THE DILIGENT STUDENT

The Diligent Student is, on the surface, a model student. They take careful notes, they do what they're told, and they always submit any homework on time. They will leave the lesson structure up to you to decide ('You're the teacher, you're the expert'), and they obediently trust your assessments.

But when you scratch the surface, they may have a Hero character, and/or maybe a Self-Sacrificer character. This means that the challenge for them (and for you as a teacher) will be their motivation levels, as they are likely to be external rather than internal. If their external motivation plunges, they will find it hard to keep going. Therefore, try and stimulate their internal motivation. You can do this by exploring their personal interests, by making them feel that they are in control of their language journey and encouraging them to set their own goals.

THE GRAMMAR NERD

The Grammar Nerd loves grammar. The more complicated, the better. They thrive on discussing intricate details of grammar and go deep into exceptions and maybe even etymology. A Grammar Nerd may enjoy spending hours and hours talking *about* the language but feel very out of depth when it comes to practical applications, like speaking.

You shouldn't be surprised if there's a Hero character somewhere inside a Grammar Nerd. They are likely to thrive on feeling intelligent and clever. Pay attention to whether you think their motivation is external only, or also internal. If the Grammar Nerd experiences truly internal motivation by being curious and feeling satisfied when they've learned something, you don't have to worry so much about their motivation levels. But if their motivation is mainly external, then you need to watch out in the same way as with any Diligent Student, and help them build up a stronger internal motivation level. Encourage them to actually *use* the language more, rather than just talking about it!

THE NERVOUS PERFECTIONIST

This character can take many different forms. The Nervous Perfectionist may be terrified of opening their mouth to speak, as they feel so worried about saying something incorrectly. They may beat themselves up regarding their pronunciation, writing, reading comprehension, or listening skills. They may minimize their achievements ('I'm not good enough', 'I still can't…') and get stuck in minute details of their language production, which means they rarely achieve any sense of flow. When I meet Nervous Perfectionists, I feel the voices in their heads are so loud that I'm sometimes unsure of whom I'm speaking to!

As you have probably already figured out, the Nervous Perfectionist is dominated by the Judge and the Victim. Therefore, your biggest challenge as a teacher of a Nervous Perfectionist is to challenge their inner Judge. Before you've started to challenge their Judge, it can be quite difficult to make any kind of progress, because they are riddled with self-doubt. Having an open discussion about their fears, and showing examples of typical language-learning myths will help them to start distancing themselves from their Judge. If you want (I have done this several times), you can even talk about the Judge character and explain what they might sound like and why they're not helpful when learning a language. You could ask them to name their Judge (for fun), and playfully call them out when you hear their Judge speaking.

THE CLOCK-IN CLOCK-OUT

The Clock-In Clock-Out character is one who pays for their lessons but does nothing else in-between lessons. They won't do any homework and won't take any personal responsibility for their learning. They may have many excuses ('work has been crazy', 'family matters', 'slept poorly', 'didn't have time', etc.), and they also have an attitude of expecting progress as a direct result of having paid for time with you. It's transactional for them, as if they expect the knowledge to be imported into their brain by just sitting in front of you. You may feel that you're 'child-minding' them during lessons.

There can certainly be an element of the Entitled character here. There may be a sense of entitlement that has created the transactional perspective on learning. The Clock-In Clock-Out student may be used to solving problems by throwing money at them. It could also be that they have a Saboteur that encourages procrastination. In my experience, it may also be due to a complete lack of knowledge about how learning actually works. It could be that they *simply* haven't realized that they are the ones that need to do the majority of the work when it comes to language learning, and that you can't just install a piece of software into their brains. Therefore, your focus here will be to teach them how to learn, before teaching them the language itself. Help them build study routines, give them tools (trackers, planners, checklists), and talk about planning their weekly study routine outside of lessons.

If you don't help them realize this, they can become disappointed in their lack of progress over time. A typical comment along these lines could sound like this:

> 'I don't feel like I've progressed, even though I've been having lessons with you now for x months/years.'

What they fail to realize is that perhaps they have only had, say, ten hourly lessons with you over x months/years, and they have done no practice themselves in that time. So essentially, they've had less than two days' worth of an intensive course, but they choose to measure it in months/years (which sounds like slow progress). This is something you definitely want to avoid, as it can damage your reputation and lead to negative reviews. The way to do this is to hammer home the fact that you measure language learning 'time' in hours spent studying (lesson hours + outside of lesson hours), and not in calendar weeks/months/years. What does 'six months' mean, really? It could be ten hours, or it could be 650 hours, which of course is a huge difference.

This will help the Clock-In Clock-Out student to create a more realistic view of their language-learning process, take more personal responsibility, and you will avoid them being disappointed by any lack of progress due to their own lack of priorities.

THE HAPPY BUT SLOPPY SPEAKER

The Happy but Sloppy Speaker is a fun student character who loves to hear their own voice. They're enthusiastic, unafraid and enjoyable to spend time with. But, they want to run before they can walk, and they have no time for grammar structure and 'boring rules'. Grammar is uninspiring, and they just 'want to talk'. Because of this attitude, they have adopted many bad habits, and you may often hear their mother tongue coming through in their speech (especially in small filler words, like 'well', 'but', 'so', 'like'). They are unlikely to even notice this, as their infectious enthusiasm has led to few people correcting their speech. They are the complete opposite of the Nervous Perfectionist.

This student character may harbour one or more of the characters of drama: the Villain (the Rebel and/or the Saboteur) and the Entitled. The Rebel character may lie beneath their perception of grammar; their Rebel may not want to follow rules. Or if they have a clear Saboteur, it could be that the lack of attention to grammar and structure comes from procrastination. If they have an Entitled character, it may say to them that they are 'above' having to learn grammar, and they are justified in just 'having fun'. In order to get to the bottom of how to help this type of student to progress, you will need to figure out what the dominant character is first, and then tackle that.

THE RESOLUTION BREAKER

Usually in January, the Resolution Breaker books in lessons with you. They can turn up at any point of the year, but they are most likely to start early in the year. They are extremely motivated, pumped even, and will communicate intensively with you before they start. They will fork out money on a package straight away and talk about how they will now *really focus* on their language learning. They may have tried to learn for a long time, on and off, and may have a partner who's a native speaker. They will start out enthusiastically but are likely to cool off after a few months.

Characters that could be found in the Resolution Breaker are the Judge and the Saboteur. It could be that they have a strong Judge telling them that they 'should' learn the language. They may feel that they should learn because of people around them (partners, parents, colleagues, friends, etc.), meaning their motivation is mainly external. Their Judge could also quietly whisper in their ear that they are not good enough, slowly breaking down their confidence over time. They may also have a Saboteur that tells them to postpone and to procrastinate. They may feel that it's 'too hard', so they start to skip homework, skip lessons, and then they feel they are not making any progress so they give up. It's therefore important to stimulate their internal motivation, and also encourage them to set up a realistic study routine that they can follow, which can carry them through if/when their motivation starts to dwindle.

THE CREATIVE AND SELF-SUFFICIENT

Occasionally, you'll come across the Creative and Self-Sufficient. This is a student who has a beautiful balance between being creative, studious, self-motivated, meticulous, open, realistic but also curious. They take responsibility for their own learning yet listen to your advice. When you teach them something, they will immediately try and incorporate it into their production of the language. And when you introduce something new (for example, a new grammar rule), they will explore it further on their own after the lesson. They will try new things out and come to you for feedback. They will explore new tools, seek out new resources, and they will balance the need for thorough grammar knowledge with creative language production. They will not beat themselves up when they make mistakes, and they are not afraid to try new things. They will plan their own study routines and they will make steady progress, as they will make sure they put in the necessary regular hours to reach their milestones. They don't seem to have any dominant characters in their heads, and you'll enjoy every second you spend with them.

OTHER INFLUENCING FACTORS

It's also worth mentioning that many other factors can influence students' ability and capacity to learn a new language. Learning differences like dyslexia, or differences like ADHD and autism, as well as many types of mental health issues, can impact on a student's ability to do certain things. Sometimes, adult students may not be aware that they have such differences, and it's not our job as language teachers to diagnose them. But it's good to be aware that such factors can also play a role in their learning journey, and I have found it useful to explore learning preferences with each student. Even if they don't know their preferred learning modes (some may have never thought about how they best learn), it can be useful to raise the awareness of the fact that there are many different ways of learning. You can encourage the student to explore various learning strategies. There is more than one way to learn a language!

What your student wants or what your student needs?

Help your students to set some realistic goals, so they can feel a sense of progress as they are studying with you. What people need depends on how they want to use the language. Someone studying to pass an exam in order to apply for education or a job will require different things from someone who wants to be able to write emails to a friend or relative. But it also depends on what character they are. Your job as a Language Teacher Rebel is to recognize their characters, but also to challenge them and inspire them.

It can be easy sometimes to just 'give them what they want' (for example, giving a Grammar Nerd lots of grammar knowledge). But if you gently challenge them, their journey will be so much more rewarding for you both. By recognizing their comfort zones and their characters, you can help to guide your students towards expanding their knowledge, and hopefully moving outside of their comfort zones, so they can achieve their language goals and even experience something they had not expected. If you do this, they will become your biggest fans.

Teaching language skills

LISTENING

Listening skills are so important. Yet, in my experience, they are often forgotten by teachers as well as by students. Many students tell me they would like to communicate better, but what they usually mean is they want to speak better and with more confidence. What they often forget is that if they don't understand what someone is saying, their speaking skills don't matter.

Listening practice lends itself nicely to homework, as it's something that the student can do on their own. That is, if they actually do it. It can be useful to do some listening exercises together during a session first, to make sure the student understands what you're asking them to do. Or record an instruction video that you can send the student, that shows exactly how to do it.

If you're teaching using a course book, it's likely that the book will include access to audio clips. If so, use them as they come up, and set them as homework. You can ask the student to listen and answer some listening comprehension questions (if there are no questions in the course book, you can create some). If you have a more advanced student, you can ask them to listen to a radio programme or a podcast, which you can then discuss during your next lesson. The student can go deeper with their listening practice through pronunciation analysis and transcriptions.

Pronunciation analysis involves a student listening repeatedly to a text or dialogue while simultaneously looking at the written version, and marking what the pronunciation sounds like. This could include crossing out letters that aren't pronounced, marking letter combinations that are pronounced in a particular way, or marking how words are combined and/or stressed in speech. This kind of analysis will help the student gain confidence and overcome the bridge between how the language is written and how it's spoken. As a bonus, it will indirectly also help to improve their pronunciation, as the student will pay close attention to what the language actually sounds like when natives speak, which they can start to copy.

Transcription requires the student to listen to an audio clip without seeing the written text, while writing down what they hear word for word. This will take a long time to do, as the student will need to pause and go back many times throughout the exercise. Therefore, make sure you don't give them long audio clips to transcribe. Thirty seconds or a minute will do. When they have written it down as best as they can, they need to compare the written text with what they have written. But not just that, they need to analyse why they may have missed things in the audio clip. Was it because the pronunciation was not what they expected? Perhaps it was a new word they didn't know? Or was it a case of words running into each other, making several words sound like one? By doing this detailed analysis, the student will start to improve their listening skills quickly. It may be useful to do the comparison and the analysis together with the student the first time, so they understand the importance of these steps and also how to do it.

SPEAKING

When you teach adults, in my experience at least, the thing they want to do the most is converse in their target language. You may need to help them to set some realistic goals, as sometimes beginners believe that just ten or so lessons will enable them to master speaking on a B2 level of the CEFR. They may not refer to B2, but when you scratch the surface, they may want to hold a conversation with a native about almost any topic without strain for either party (which is one of the criteria for B2).

Beginners

Introduce a few key sentences and phrases that you can always begin each session with ('Hello, how are you?', 'I'm good thanks, and you?'). This will build their confidence as they get to practise the same thing every time you begin a session. You can also introduce a few 'outro' sentences and phrases that you always use before hanging up. So even if they can't speak much otherwise, and you'll spend the session teaching vocabulary or grammar, they can at least begin to use these phrases automatically.

Another useful step is to introduce a couple of past-tense verbs and create a couple of sentences around those. This makes that first target-language interaction a bit longer ('What did you do last weekend?/How was your weekend?', 'I went to…', 'We watched…', 'I met up with…', 'I worked…').

I find that language course books often start by introducing the present tense first, followed by the infinitive and the imperative perhaps, and much later the past tense. I can understand from a grammatical building-block type of perspective how this makes sense, but from a practical point of view, it's just not that useful. Learning how to say your name and where you're from is all good in one way, but to be honest, we don't introduce ourselves to someone that often. And we only tend to do it once! A lot of the conversations that my students throughout the years have wanted to master are those social, everyday exchanges with friends, extended family or colleagues.

Without being too philosophical about it, when we talk, we often talk in the past or in the future. We are rarely in the present. Therefore, even if my students are following a more traditional course book, I always introduce these types of exchanges as early as possible. The students can dip their toe into a bit of past tense, for example, without having to learn the whole grammatical foundation of it. And when they reach that level in a course, they have already tried it in practice, so it becomes easier to digest.

Intermediate and more advanced students

What activities you choose will depend on what they are trying to achieve, and what characters they are. If you have a Nervous Perfectionist or a Grammar Nerd on your hands, you can build up their confidence in speaking by gentle improvisation that focuses on the interaction, rather than perfect grammar. Don't over-correct them. Instead, show genuine interest in what they are telling you, ask many follow-up questions, and praise them often. Point out to them that they are doing great when they've achieved even the smallest amount of 'flow' in their speech. Reassure them that the most important thing is to be understood and to be able to communicate, rather than being 'perfect'.

If you have a Happy but Sloppy Speaker as your student, you can try and frame any speaking practice around specific grammar constructions and encourage them to slow down their speech (they're usually fast speakers). Nip their bad habits in the bud and push them in a friendly but firm way to tighten up their speech.

You can choose to freely improvise (as you would speak to a friend, perhaps while introducing idioms and more informal slang expressions). This might feel a bit unstructured, as if you're not really teaching. But remember that this is often the kind of everyday conversation that students want to be able to master.

You can also set a specific topic, perhaps in advance, so the student can research some keywords beforehand and prepare to speak on this topic. Typical topics might be culture, food, travel, work, studies, hobbies and free time, money, health, IT and technology, the environment, and family and relationships. You can set topic questions that prompt the student to compare options/cultures or argue a specific point. If you want inspiration for questions, you could search for B2 exam questions online. Or you could search for questions to ask on a first date! Keep a document somewhere with a list of topics and questions, so you can easily access them when you need them.

READING

Reading is often perceived as the easiest of tasks for students. This is because it isn't done in real time (like listening) and it's not focusing on production (like speaking). Keep a folder in your digital library with reading resources (or links to them online). If you're using a course book, there should be plenty of content there. It's fun and motivating to use additional resources, like newspaper articles, books and blog posts.

Ask your student to read a text out loud during a lesson and give feedback on their pronunciation and prosody (intonation, stress and rhythm). You can read the text first, followed by the student reading it. Or they can read it first while you guide them through the text, and correct them where needed. After that, ask them to translate the text and go through any new words with them (meaning, word category and any grammar details). Encourage them to note the new words down and practise them as homework for next time. You can also encourage them to use a flashcard program to practise new words (such as Anki, Quizlet or Wokabulary). After that, you can ask comprehension questions on the text, prompting them to answer by looking at the text.

If your student is a bit more advanced, you can set them as homework to read (and perhaps translate) a specific text or a section from a book, identify and look up any new words, and prepare to talk about it next time. Find out from your student what they're interested in, so you can find texts relating to their interests and passions. This is particularly helpful for students who exhibit high levels of external motivation, like the Resolution Breaker, the Diligent Student or maybe the Grammar Nerd.

WRITING

Getting your students into the habit of writing regularly is a great way to get them to apply both grammar and vocabulary. Sometimes students may shy away from writing, as they feel it takes too much time (especially students like the Happy but Sloppy Speaker). I use writing exercises as a tool to identify their grammar weaknesses, and also as a way to teach them how to self-correct. I use cloud-based programs like Google Docs, so the student can view the text at the same time as I correct it and give feedback.

If you want your student to get into the habit of writing, it doesn't matter what the topic is. You can ask them to simply write some diary entries (what they did last week, what they will do next week). You can also set writing exercises as homework, attached to another exercise. They can write questions on a text you have worked on during a lesson or summarize a text in written form. If you really want to focus on tightening up grammar, you can ask your student to write grammar drills (for example, sentences where they practise a particular grammar point: 'I'm driving to work today, I drove to work yesterday, I have driven to work this week', and so on).

If your student is intermediate level or more advanced, it's good to focus on writing in different styles/voices/genres. Guide them through how to write in a formal vs informal tone and discuss the appropriate choice of words and expressions for different contexts. You can set them specific writing tasks in different contexts, for example writing an informal message to a close friend, a semi-formal email to a colleague, a letter of complaint to a company, an opinion piece for a local newspaper, and so on.

Summary

ACTION PLAN

- Set up student folders.
- Create digital copies of teaching materials.
- Create digital copies and links for extra resources.
- Be aware of different student types and their needs.
- Help your students to set realistic goals.

Checklist

Here's a useful checklist of the summaries and action plans from each chapter that you can use to track your Language Teacher Rebel set-up journey.

Chapter 1

The Digital Age presents a huge number of opportunities for both language students and language teachers.

It's not too late to start teaching online.

Your varied experiences are your strengths.

You will have a lot of flexibility as a Language Teacher Rebel. Think about how you would like to design your days and your work-week.

Becoming a Language Teacher Rebel offers a mission to support integration and cultural understanding.

Chapter 2

- [ ] Working on your mindset is one of the most important things to do as you become a business owner.
- [ ] Explore your mindset continuously, especially around work and money, with a non-judgmental and accepting attitude.
- [ ] Surround yourself with people who inspire you.
- [ ] Get to know your common fears so you can recognize when they visit you.
- [ ] Take steps to build your confidence and develop your intuition.

Chapter 3

☐ Create a new opportunity, not an improvement offer.

☐ Choose a service or product that you want to create, based on how they compare in the different categories, and package it nicely.

☐ Teaching live one-to-one is the easiest way to start.

☐ Remember that 'online' doesn't mean a low price.

☐ Aim to eventually create a Product Ecosystem, including:

- a First Free Offer
- an Intro Product
- a Core Product
- a Product for Clients.

Chapter 4

☐ Identify your micro-niche by examining submarkets and niches.

☐ Listen in online to what people's difficulties and problems are.

☐ Create your why-statement.

☐ Explore your Culture Add.

☐ Craft a pitch.

☐ Take every opportunity to practise your pitch; you never know when an opportunity will come your way.

Chapter 5

The Language Teacher Rebel Roadmap includes the following five steps:

- ☐ The Quick Tech Set Up
- ☐ The Quick Marketing Material Creation Blitz
- ☐ Early Growth – Evolving and Engaging
- ☐ Developing and Investing
- ☐ Flourishing with Momentum

Chapter 6

- ☐ Set up an email address.
- ☐ Set up an email program.
- ☐ Set up teaching tools.
- ☐ Set up a social media channel.
- ☐ Set up a payment tool.
- ☐ Set up a booking system (which could be a free account to start with).

Chapter 7

- ☐ Create a Lead Magnet.
- ☐ Create Pillar Content.
- ☐ Create content upgrades.
- ☐ Create content about yourself.
- ☐ Plan your content creation by sprinting and batching, and using a content calendar.

☐ Be clear about who your ideal student is and start hanging out where they hang out. Provide value and be helpful. No promotion.

Chapter 8

☐ Get familiar and start playing with tools for creating video and visual content.

☐ Schedule posts for social media, and foster a community where members are encouraged to participate and interact.

☐ Think about how you want to use your email list in order to keep it warm.

☐ Gather reviews and publish them.

Chapter 9

☐ Upgrade to a paid plan on your online booking system, if you haven't already.

☐ Develop your website.

☐ Consider whether you want to have a blog.

☐ Optimize your website to make it easier for search engines to find it.

Chapter 10

☐ Consider starting to record videos, if you haven't already. Practice makes perfect.

- [ ] Develop partnerships with vertical marketing partners, through a 'courting process' via social media. Don't be discouraged if a partnership is not formed immediately.
- [ ] Set up systems and processes to free up more of your time.
- [ ] Remember that bookings can be cyclical. Spend quiet periods designing and developing products and services that add to your Product Ecosystem.
- [ ] Creating a new offer is a good way to give yourself a pay rise.
- [ ] Start thinking of things you could outsource.
- [ ] Plan holiday, weeks 'off' and daily breaks to maintain a healthy work–life balance.

Chapter 11

- [ ] Set up student folders.
- [ ] Create digital copies of teaching materials.
- [ ] Create digital copies and links for extra resources.
- [ ] Be aware of different student types and their needs.
- [ ] Help your students to set realistic goals.

Glossary

Automation A system where one or more processes happen automatically. In this context, it may be a system enabling your students or prospective students to receive certain things (information, offers, etc.) or access certain things (booking calendar, online courses, payment options, etc.) automatically.

Batching A method of planning tasks, where you do similar tasks at the same time.

Blended course An online course that also includes live sessions.

Cloud computing File-hosting systems that offer cloud storage and file synchronization.

Content upgrade A free download that you attach/link to a blog post (or offer as part of a presentation or interview, for example).

Core market A big market such as health, finance or outdoor activities, for example.

Culture Add A statement that describes what makes you unique in your business, taking into account your background, your identity, your circumstances, your experiences and your beliefs.

Domain name The address that people type in the browser URL bar to visit a website.

Email list A collection of email addresses, from people who have opted in to your email list, kept in an email list program.

GDPR (General Data Protection Regulation) A regulation in EU law on data protection and privacy in the European Union (EU) and the European Economic Area (EEA). It also addresses the transfer of personal data outside the EU and EEA areas.

Improvement offer Offering a slightly better version of what someone else already offers; this can be harder to sell.

Landing page A single web page that appears in response to clicking on a marketing email, an online advertisement, or a search result link. The general goal of a landing page is to convert site visitors into sales or leads (for example by encouraging visitors to join an email list).

Lead magnet Something that you'll give away for free in exchange for an email address, for example an e-book, a free email course, or a pre-recorded webinar/video lesson.

Micro-niche A very small market within a niche, for example arthritis diets for vegans, or environmentally friendly campervan designs.

New opportunity offer Offering something new, replacing what hasn't worked in the past; this can be easier to sell.

Niche A smaller market within a submarket; weight loss for parents, for example, or campervan conversion services.

Opt-in The process used to describe when a positive action is required in order to subscribe a user to an email list.

Outsourcing Allocating certain tasks to someone else.

Pillar Content Key articles that are part of the foundation for your business.

Procrasti-planning Planning as a way of avoiding taking action, leading to a false sense of being productive.

Product Ecosystem A system of offers that includes a free offer, a low-cost offer (Intro Product), a high-cost offer (Core Product) and a continuation offer (Product for Clients). The offers should all support each other and work seamlessly together.

SEO (Search Engine Optimization) The process of improving the quality and quantity of website traffic to a website or a web page from search engines.

Spring planning A method of planning where you break bigger projects down into smaller chunks that you can complete in two weeks, during which time you only focus on completing that part of the project.

SSL (Secure Sockets Layer) A form of security technology. It's a protocol for servers and web browsers that makes sure that data passed between the two are private. This is done using an encrypted link that connects the server and browser. You can see that a website has SSL certification if the website address begins with 'https' instead of just 'http'.

Subcontracting Having someone working for you who sends an invoice for the hours they have worked (or for the cost of the project).

Submarket A smaller market within a core market, for example weight loss or campervan travel.

Webhosting A service provided by companies (the web hosts) that sell or lease space on a server where you store the files that make your website accessible on the internet.

References

Brunson, R., *Expert Secrets: The Underground Playbook for Creating a Mass Movement of People Who Will Pay for Your Advice*. Narrated by Hank Bannister (Audible, 2017) [Audiobook].

Kennedy, Shannon, 'Applying the Minimalist Approach To Language Learning', Eurolinguiste (2017) <http://eurolinguiste.com/applying-minimalist-approach-language-learning/>, accessed 25 May 2020.

Kim, W., Chan and Mauborgne, Renee, *Blue Ocean Strategy, Expanded Edition: How to Create Uncontested Market Space and Make the Competition Irrelevant* (Boston: Harvard Business Review Press, 2006).

Mariah Coz Show https://mariahcoz.com/blog/tag/Podcast, accessed 15 April 2020.

Pariser, E., 'Beware online 'filter bubbles' [video], *TED*, March 2011. https://www.ted.com/talks/eli_pariser_beware_online_filter_bubbles, accessed 12 March 2019.

Priestley, D., *Entrepreneur Revolution: How to Develop your Entrepreneurial Mindset and Start a Business that Works* (Chichester: Capstone Publishing Ltd, 2013).

Sinek, S., 'How great leaders inspire action' [video], *TED*, Sep 2009. https://www.ted.com/talks/simon_sinek_how_great_leaders_inspire_action, accessed 20 March 2019.

Sutherland, J.J., *Scrum: The Art of Doing Twice the Work in Half the Time* (Redfern, New South Wales: Currency Press, 2014).

Van Warmerdam, G., *MindWorks: A Practical Guide for Changing Thoughts, Beliefs, and Emotional Reactions* (Santa Barbara, California: Cairn Publishing, 2014).